The Jig is Up: We Are One!

Race is a Hoax that FAILS American Education

JOHNNIE P. MITCHELL

*To President Biden
Please bring the
HUMAN family back
together!*

*Johnnie
5/26/21*

iUniverse, Inc.
New York Bloomington

iUniverse books may be ordered through booksellers or by contacting:

iUniverse
1663 Liberty Drive
Bloomington, IN 47403
www.iuniverse.com
1-800-Authors (1-800-288-4677)

Because of the dynamic nature of the Internet, any Web addresses or links contained in this book may have changed since publication and may no longer be valid. The views expressed in this work are solely those of the author and do not necessarily reflect the views of the publisher, and the publisher hereby disclaims any responsibility for them.

ISBN: 978-1-4502-1986-0 (sc)
ISBN: 978-1-4502-1990-7 (hc)
ISBN: 978-1-4502-1988-4 (ebook)

Printed in the United States of America

iUniverse rev. date: 04/16/2010

TABLE OF CONTENTS

The Educational "R" - evolution

How to Restart Education in a Non-Racial America

PREFACE

- I started collecting the information for this book approximately twenty-five years ago and always felt it wasn't quite the right time for the "book"
- It turns out I couldn't have written this particular book without the information I have obtained as recently as this week, (the week of January 20, 2009)
- Now is the time, I can join the "age of responsibility" by sharing the information in this book that I hope will instill the "passion for education" that my people embraced as they left life as slaves and became free Americans. That same passion for education is needed right now and I think that it is my responsibility to share some things that I know with my beloved America as we continue on our journey to becoming a great nation!
- As a very spiritual person, I now appreciate everything that I have experienced in my life as preparation for this book/ movement.
- May the spirit of my ancestors be with all of you as you read this book!

In the Beginning was the Word … "Restart Education"

Over fifteen years ago I got this passion to do something about the state of education in America. The mantra became "restart education." I wasn't even sure if "restart" was a word but being the rebel that I am, I accepted it as a word even if it wasn't.

Now seems to be the time, the country has caught up, everywhere we see or hear, renew, restore, refuel, restart is everywhere now, "re" is the theme in America today!

That's how it started. That was ten years after "*A Nation-at-Risk, 1983*" came out and then "reform" was everywhere. Well, ten years later it was obvious to me that rearranging the chairs on the Titanic was not doing anything good for anybody.

I knew my biggest problem was going to be getting anybody to pay attention to me, a poor Black woman with a lot of guts. I even drew a picture of my challenge: the scene is where everybody is on the highway following the lead car, the important people, the White people or wealthy Black people and there I was at the back of the line waving, I've got a different idea, please pay attention to me! How was I ever going to get anybody to pay attention to me?

The other picture was of me in a small boat (bateau) and I was out in front of the *Titanic*-sized education system trying to get the "ship" to turn around ...

Well, fifteen years later and my beloved America has fallen off a cliff ...

I think it's time to "Restart Education in America" and there are some truths that we have to know before we can do it right!

PURPOSE OF THIS BOOK

This book is written to help save our country and consequently save our world. A gigantic hoax was played on America called "race."

This book is going to bring forth truth and honesty in our country as we move forward from the financial meltdown that our country has suffered.

While America became the greatest country in the world, it still needs to strive to become a great nation. (In my opinion, America can never be great until it deals honestly with race)

Race and racism have played a significant role in the rise and fall of America.

This book will chronicle the history of "race" in America.

It will start with how the concept of "race" was constructed. It will proceed with the history of race to justify slavery of Blacks and grant superiority privileges to Whites.

How it has been used to take America to greatness for the benefit of one group (Whites) and on the backs of the other group (Blacks) will be provided.

The "jig is up" – the trick or game is finished, has been exposed, we're ready to face the truth of our past, present and future!

The book then invites you to a "non racial America." It's now about being "smart" and that is not determined by a concept of race.

While White people might be pulling the wool over Black people; that's irrelevant now; when the rest of the world is surpassing us in learning and knowledge.

Contriving a system for Whites to be permanently smarter than Black people has reached the "law of diminishing returns!"

The book concludes with "The Plan" on how to restart education to survive and thrive in a smart and successful non-racial America!

DEDICATION

This book and movement is dedicated to:

- The spirits of my ancestors
- Lucinda Patterson, Mama, for instilling in me a love for "learning"
- John Patterson, Papa, for teaching me that love comes in many forms
- John (Melanie) and Cindy (Amichai), my children for allowing me to instill in them a love for "learning"
- Hannah and Jared, my grandchildren and the others who will come
- James for keeping the family together
- Friends and partners who kept me going
- Last but not least, Ormsby Mitchel, a "White" man from Kentucky who taught my people the "value of education" as they were about to join America as a free people following the Civil War

WARNING!!!

The message in this book is true. What you have believed to be true will be shown to be absolutely false, wrong and now very bad for your well-being and the well-being of your children.

It will have the effect similar to finding out there is no Santa Claus, no tooth fairy, no Easter Bunny, your parents are not your real parents and a command to immediately learn a new language or you will be speaking a language that no one else will be speaking, at one time, from one book.

Smart people who adapt to change will make things happen quickly, others will doubt the validity of the information and will consequently watch things happens, and the ones who don't read about it will wonder what happened when they wake up one morning from a nightmare that shakes them up that the President of the United States is Black and so is the First Lady. Oh, that's already happened! Well, what about the "nightmare" that China owns our country and is contemplating not extending more credit to America. Oh, that's already real! What about the nightmare that America's children are not in the top ten of the other industrialized countries. Oh, America is actually in the bottom tier!

This book will wake you up, shake you up, and get you in the mood for some serious teaching and learning.

If you haven't let the lies kill you, the truth will certainly make you very well …

Truth Crushed to Earth Shall Rise Again

Our beloved America reached its greatness on the foundation of a big lie. Now is the time to know the truth to set us free to follow the words of our new leader President Barack Obama, let's restore America to true greatness.

Are you ready to learn the truth?

Are You Ready to Learn?

Reading this book is going to challenge your world!

It's going to present facts that you probably didn't know. There will be many things said that you will have to research for yourself. You will be challenged to research truth for yourself.

Things will be stated that you have heard before and no credit will be given. That will be your responsibility to verify or document.

This is a radical book that stares status quo in the eyes!

If you are daring enough to "learn" for yourself, come along for the greatest adventure of your intellectual life. Bring others with you.

Socrates says: "There is only one good, knowledge, and one evil, ignorance"

Let the ADVENTURE begin...

Why I am the Author

I believe that all souls come programmed for this human experience. Therefore I am the person who was destined to write this book. As in the movie, "*Slumdog Millionaire*," the hero's life experiences gave him all of the answers he needed to win the game; my personal experiences have offered me the opportunity to acquire the information and the insight that I am able to present for a time such as this ...

Listed below are some of the things I believe have happened for a particular reason and has something to do with me becoming the author of this book. The particular things that I am able to comprehend are as follows:

- Being born on Hilton Head Island to John and Lucinda Patterson in 1946 when Hilton Head was almost exclusively inhabited by Blacks and only a few Whites
- Being born into a family where "education" on both sides of the family was valued as much as life itself
- Being a descendent of Ormsby Mitchel's Town of Mitchelville where the "experiment in education" for freedmen was begun
- Attending the most deprived schools to receive excellent preparation for higher education and the value of "teaching and learning"
- Attending Spelman College, a Black college and studying under the late Dr. O. Eagleston to learn the "truth" about the bell curve and intelligence testing
- Teaching in the segregated Black schools
- Teaching at the "integrated" schools under a White controlled school system
- Being introduced to the belief of the Baha'i faith that "science and religion must agree" – if God created one people, why does "science" have different "races"
- Researching and keeping an ear open for the understanding of how more than one race could be reconciled with the unity of humanity?

- Having two children, one classified as "gifted and talented" and the other as "average" by school system tests and the effect of the classification on their education and development
- Watching the changes after Brown v. Board of Education and the lack of progress of poor Black people, particularly children
- Dissecting the "A Nation-at-Risk, 1983" like a gift from God
- As a keen observer of the Reform Movement watching the reforms mistakenly directed to the at-risk population defined as the poor Black students and keeping track of the "progress"
- Receiving a copy of the 25th anniversary of A Nation at-risk and regretfully gaining affirmation of all of my beliefs and calculations
- Becoming a historian of my Gullah/Geechee inheritance and the role of education for the success of poor Black people
- Having my son marry a White woman and having grandchildren from that union and the difference of their reality in America from their White mother
- Having my daughter marry a young man from Israel and expecting a grandchild and the reality of "race" that will be waiting for my grandchild's future
- Hearing the new Secretary of Education Arne Duncan state on CNN that our students rank #31 but we have the #1 school system in the World – that we are still suffering from a delusion that keeps us in a wrong direction of change - we still cannot face our true status (#31) so we deny the reality and buy into an illusion or self-deception (#1) that continues to keep us from doing anything about our educational system.

The Irony of the "Conversation on Race"

Are you a racist?

I have noticed that in America no one wants to be a "racist" –

While more than ever, the anticipation of the big conversation on race, looms before us, the conversation I raise is, "Do you know, there are no 'races'? Can you embrace the theory that there is only one race, the human race? Can you give up the notion that there is a 'White race' and a 'Black race'?"

Are you ready to give up your status as a White person or a Black person in America?

If you still believe in "races" then are you ready to accept the fact that you are a "racist?"

Are you White, Black or Human?

Can we finally define a "racist?"

A racist is one who believes in "races!"

Are you a "racist?"

LET THE CONVERSATION BEGIN …

INTRODUCTION

The Jig is Up!
-We Are One-
How to Restart Education in a Non-Racial America

Welcome to the greatest adventure in learning that I hope you have ever taken or ever will take! Let's begin the adventure with the meaning of the title, "The Jig is Up!" Literally this phrase suggests that the dance is over and that the time has come to pay the fiddler. However, the meaning of the expression has evolved and the derivative precisely explains the interpretation of the meaning that relates to the appropriateness of the title for this adventure.

While 'Jig' is a very old term for a lively dance, later in Elizabethan times, the word became slang for a practical joke or a trick. "The jig is up" – means your trick or game is finished, has been exposed, we're onto you now. "Jig" is also a racial slur, a derogatory term for a Black man. Ragtime piano was called "jig piano" and the syncopating bands, like Scott Joplin's were called "jig bands." This term, taken from jig dances, even came a little later to be a designation for the Black man himself. (For a bit of humor, the Black sheriff, played by Cleavon Little, in the Mel Brooks' movie, *Blazing Saddles*, did a little wordplay with the two unrelated phrases in the line: "The jig is up, and GONE.")

The message that is being presented in this book is that the "The Jig is up, and it's time to MOVE ON!" Some of you may remember a very popular book, **Who Moved My Cheese.** In that book when the mice realized that the source of their sustenance (cheese) was gone, some refused to believe that could happen and others immediately understood the ramification and went in search of another source. In essence the book is about the variety of reactions to change.

This book is very much like that. This book chronicles the history of race in America, as a hoax or trick and how that hoax served a purpose and now the trick helps no one and we need to move on together. The time has come for a new way, for a new day and that means the American education system that is based (race-based, bell-curve testing standards) on the hoax must be restarted for the benefit of all (America and the World).

I feel a tremendous responsibility to share the information I have on where we are, how we got here, and how to move forward to restore our country. As I approached the writing of this book, I was faced with a daunting or haunting question, "How will I be able to convince a nation to listen to me and to adopt a new paradigm for our educational system?"

When "A Nation-at-Risk" came out in 1983 and gave Americans everything they needed to avert the meltdown of America, 2008, I realized that Americans didn't understand the warning, they truly didn't get it, that they were totally blinded by "race."

For the next twenty-five years, I watched as all of the reforms were devoted to a designated, at-risk population that became synonymous with the poor, Black, urban, or rural population. White people in power didn't seem to understand, or ignored, or were just incapable of comprehending the truth of the report which was actually talking about "White-Majority" children.

The bell curve standards, I believe, blinded them to the reality that that report could be talking about "superior White people." Because they didn't know anything about the "inferior group" that their twenty-five years of reform was directed, no one has benefited. When the 25th anniversary of A Nation-at-Risk came out, it did not make the news and no commentary was made that the problem twenty-five years ago was now approximately twenty-five times worst.

Now America is much further behind the rest of the world than it was in 1983 and America is at a crossroads, lost in an economic meltdown, and no one seems to see the relationship between "race" and the impact it has on the educational system that is ultimately failing America.

My past and the history of my people's past give me hope, courage and the audacity to believe that it is possible for this book to make a difference regarding the direction and well being of our country. Putting it more specifically, if my ancestors could have endured slavery, endured the enforcement of "inferiority" for centuries, and I can sit here today, free, using a computer, I can believe that I must do my part to save my country and the World of humanity as a participant in an ever advancing civilization.

The blues singer, Bessie Smith, once sang:

It's a long road, but it's got to find an end.

I picked up my bags, and I tried it again…

After so many setbacks at so many intersections, Blacks have picked up their bags and tried, again and again, to go down the road in search of their rights as human beings. The struggle has always been to become equal citizens, to be included, within the majesty of the phrase, "We the People." Blacks and their allies have been at that pursuit for centuries and are still at it today.

I will make my case that we have got to change our educational system if we are going to turn this economy around. We allowed "ignorance" to consume us because we got caught up in a "lie" that fixated us on the notion and belief that doing better than Black people is all that matters.

Using a "bell curve" standard for testing will continue to spiral us down to the bottom of the world in terms of the level of education that is necessary for today!

For people born before the Civil Rights Movement, this book will be considered a bad joke, something to be dismissed, debated, and given its proper disposal. My hope is that the young people who have not been sold the "myth" or the "hoax" and understands that something is terribly wrong with this country right now, that a "change" is critical and they are able to be rational and understand the premise I propose. It is my hope that the "case" I present is so compelling that they may dismiss the "history" I offer but will embrace the section on how to "restart education to survive and thrive in a non-racial America."

The book is divided into two parts. The first part will concentrate on the beginning of "race-ism" and how it strangled our educational system. The second part focuses on the restarting of an educational system that has completely different goals and objectives and how to achieve those now that "we are one."

PART 1

History of Racism and How It Fails America Today

The first section is presented in "Lessons, Lessons 1-10."

When the founding fathers of our country decided to enslave a group of people, the Africans, a terrible hoax was played on everyone involved.

White people in power felt a need to permanently separate the enslaved from the enslavers by creating the myth of "race." Americans eventually became "Black" and "White." The difference in color and other physical features made it easy and lasting.

Justifying the enslavement of one group was made easier if it was "scientific" that one group was "superior" and the other group was "inferior" then the rationalization could/would become established for all times.

After hundreds of years of "conditioning" for both groups, the hoax was perpetrated, and repeated so many times that everyone on both sides started believing (or acting as if they believed) it as "truth."

The government played a large and significant role in protecting the rights of the superior group and denying rights and privileges to the deemed inferior group.

At this point in the history of our country there is no time for anger, revenge, remorse or reparation, it is time for action. Our destiny is now dependent on whether we can accept truth; make the changes and MOVE ON. Let's move on, let the lessons begin ...

-Study Guide & Timeline-

History of Racism and How It Fails America Today!

Letter #1 – When I First Learned About Race

Dear Readers,

This is the hardest thing, I believe, I have ever set out to do. Watching the past presidential election cycle gives me hope that I will be able to reach my goal. My goal is to get the attention of my fellow citizens that education is still the key to our future and there are some things we have got to "understand" if we are going to be able to "restart" education in our country. I personally take it as my duty and responsibility to accomplish this task!

Since I have lived my life as a member of the "Black" race, the designated "inferior" race I will attempt to be as "objective" as that is humanly possible. At the same time I will try to express my personal encounters that will hopefully give insight to the discourse at hand.

Let me begin with what I think is the first time I came in contact with "race." When I first knew myself, I was on an island in South Carolina. My mother was a teacher in a small community school. My father was a self-employed man who did many different things to help make a living for his family.

Most of the people on our island were Black people. Occasionally a White person would come to our house and my father would turn into a little boy, he would bow his head and answer "yes sir" over and over again, no matter what the age of the White person.

I "learned" that in this world, you have to do this to **survive** in "the White man's world."

Later I learned that the reason, I started going to school so much earlier than my other classmates, was because my mother was able to get the White superintendent to give her permission to take me to school with her since she had no other means of child care. Later he would visit the school at least once a year and I got the feeling that he was "in charge of us" and what we got was dependent on his whim and he was the "boss" whom we needed to please and obey.

At an early age I "learned" the importance of education. Every summer my mother "hitchhiked" to Savannah, Georgia to attend Savannah State (a Black college) in the nearest city to the Island. We traveled by boat and then by the ferry until 1954 when a bridge came to the Island. When the White people with money "discovered" our Island we could now get a bridge.

I also knew that my mother was active in an organization, the National Association for the Advancement of Colored People, that if the White people ever found out we would be toast. She would lose her job and my father would be harassed.

Then later there was the Southern Christian Leadership Conference headed by a Dr. Martin Luther King, Jr. Somehow it related to the fact that when we went to Savannah and ate at *Kress (a five and dime store)* we had to stand up at a section where we could see the White people sit down at the lunch counter with full service.

Fast forward to rather recent times, I started hearing that there really wasn't any "race" just one race, "the human race."

At this time I will present the "research" that I have chosen to believe. This is absolutely necessary to understand why we have to "restart" our education system and how it has to be done.

For changes to take place, the people in power, the people without power, the parents and the grandparents must all do something about this "race-ism" to understand the American dilemma that is self-inflicted and consequently save our great country for the benefit of ourselves and future generations.

With much humility, I am,

Ms. Johnnie

SECTION 1
ORIGIN OF THE HOAX

Lesson #1

RACE MYTH
Made-In-America

In the beginning when I was first introduced to the concept of race, we were taught that there were three races, Black (Negroid), White (Caucasoid), Yellow (Mongoloid) and Red.

As a Black person I grew up with the understanding that the United States operated by this rule: if you are White, you are right; if you are Brown (Mixed) stick around; and if you are Black, get back!

At the inauguration of the first "Black" President, the Rev. Dr. Lowery ended his prayer asking God to bring about a change to that operational rule:

> Lord, in the memory of all the saints who from their labors rest, and in the joy of a new beginning, we ask you to help us work for that day when Black will not be asked to get in back, when Brown can stick around ... when Yellow will be mellow... when the Red man can get ahead, man; and when *White will embrace what is right.* That all those who do justice and love mercy say Amen.

My prayer is that all men will give truth a chance and walk into the marvelous light of that truth...

The Origin of the Race Myth

This is how I believe the story goes...

Once upon a time humanity started in Africa and after people traveled and settled in other areas of the planet, they started to look and act differently.

So when the Europeans began to settle America they had in place a servant system until they realized that the people in certain parts of Africa could be enslaved forever because of their distinct physical characteristics.

We must trace, learn, and understand the history and origin of "race" in America to get us to the conclusion regarding what we must do to truly reconstruct America and restart education.

In the scientific world, it is generally accepted that the biological species of man started in Africa and later different groups migrated from Africa and settled in different areas of earth. Those groups consequently developed different characteristics based on their history, culture, and geographical conditions.

When you uncover the roots of the concept of race in North America, it's the beginning of a tale or myth to rationalize, or justify the enslavement of one group of people. Since some physical characteristics of the enslaved group's, color, nose structure, feet, and hair, etc, looked like "genetic" differences; "race" was "legitimized" by 19th century "science."

When the world was divided by distance, it was easy to believe that human beings could be bundled into three or four fundamentally different groups according to their physical traits: Blacks, Whites, Asians (Yellow), and Indians (Red).

If there is anybody left who really believes that there is more than one biological or scientific "race" this is the place for you. Whether you agree or disagree you must have this understanding if you are going to be able to proceed from this point onward and the fact that America is #31 in the world in regards to "education" and after 25 years of "reform" what we have gotten is the #31 rank. Twenty-five years earlier we were approximately #5.

The *Facts about Race* as I have learned are as follows:
There is only one (1) race, and that is the "human" race.

Any other notion of race is a "myth." Americans dealing with the issue of slavery devised a "pseudoscience". Consider these concepts from *(Race-The Power of an Illusion: 3-Part documentary about race in society, science & history (www.pbs.org/race):*

1. *Race is a concept devised in recent times.* During earlier times they did not use physical characteristics to classify humans; instead they used things like religion, status, class, and in some cases language. The word 'race' turns up for the first time in England in a 1508 poem by William Dunbar.

2. *Race is only a concept and has no scientific, biological or genetic criteria.* That means that there is no one characteristic, trait or gene all the members of one so-called race have in common and different from all the members of another so-called race.

3. *There are no subspecies of the Human species. All humans belong to the species Homo sapiens sapiens.* Scientists believe that the reason for this is the fact that humans have not the conditions that would have allowed humans to divide into sub-species or "races." More specifically, humans are one of the most genetically alike than all other species.

4. *Skin color is just skin color.* This means that a person's skin color only tells you one thing, the person's skin color. Other things like blood type, talents, abilities, and eye shape have nothing to do with the skin color of a person.

5. *Variations occur to a greater degree within races rather than between so-called "races."* The occurrences of differences reveal where there is human variation, approximately 85% occur within local populations like Italians, Kurds, Koreans or Cherokees rather between groups. That means that two random Blacks could exhibit more differences than a White person and a Black person.

The facts are that there just is no characteristic that members of a "race" have that distinguishes them from another "race." If any number of characteristics or traits were assigned to a particular "race" there is no group of those traits that would correspond to America's concept of race. When you go below the skin color, the human species is one of the most homogeneous species in existence!

Among those **not considered White** at some time in American history have been the Irish, Germans, some Jews, Italians, Spaniards, Slavs, Greeks and other Mediterranean peoples.

The differences we call "race based" are socially-based. The stress of racism, access to medical care, health insurance, race-based poverty, and living conditions can certainly affect medical outcomes. But the reasons aren't innate or genetic as America is still operating.

America's adoption of the concept of "race" has allowed the country to disregard all of the social factors that have created the inequalities and differences that they want to believe are innate or natural rather than environmental.

Accepting the fact that the concept of race is a hoax is critical at this point in America's history. The concept of race is based on a pseudo-science that was constructed to justify the differences between Black people and White people. The hoax is man-made and the discrepancies are consequently man-made. Not until this fact is known and accepted, the ignorance of the lie is going to keep everyone in America from getting a good education and having a fair chance in life.

Timeline

1640 – Chattel Slavery
The term White race or White people entered dictionaries of the major European languages in the 1600s.

1680-
During this period, the laws referred to people as "Christians" or "Englishmen" and not "Whites." Then during the time of Bacon's Rebellion in 1676 there is a noticeable change which distinguishes Black slaves from European indentured servants.

The concept of "race" then becomes prevalent as status of slavery becomes an inherited status. The legal category of "White" was put into effect to institutionalize a variety of laws that gave different rights and privileges to the "races."

1705-
The institution of slavery becomes more preferred than indentured servitude for the wealthy planter. At that point they began to put on the books laws that turned African slaves into a permanent status that definitively distinguished Blacks from Whites. With Blacks being skilled, knowledgeable, possessing natural immunity to European diseases and no place to hide with their dark skins, the Africans/Blacks became the group chosen to become permanent slaves.

1735 –
The publishing of Linnaeus' *Systema Naturae* is key to this trace of the man-made creation of "races."

1758-
A Swedish botanist, physician and zoologist, Carolus Linnaeus gives White people a classification, *Homo sapiens europaeus* and for the first time attributes mental capabilities to them as a group.

1775-
The philosopher Immanuel Kant has the term "White" in book, "About the Different Races of Men" and describes them as a race or group.

In Blumenbach's *Natural Varieties of Mankind,* the "White" and "Black" race is introduced.

1776-
This is the point in time when Johann Blumenbach is credited with the originator of Caucasians/Whites. This is when he generates a template for "races." He creates hierarchical pyramid

of five human types. He placed "Caucasians" at the top because he believed that all of the other types diverged. (This belief becomes the "scientific" basis for the claim of White superiority that continues to today!)

1790-
Since the U.S. Constitution orders a census count every 10 years; racial classification is included. (At this time in history, finding out who is free and who is enslaved is more important than whether as person is Black or White- to this day, that is still what the census is trying to find out, "are you a descendent of slavery (Black) or descendent of the free (White). This is when a slave/Black person is counted as 3/5ths of a person. **(At this point in history they believe in the difference between Blacks and Whites but they attribute the difference to environment rather than inherited.)**

1899-
People brought to America from southern and Eastern Europe increase at this time. They joined the already present Africans, Mexicans and Chinese Americans doing the undesirable, low-wage jobs living in the urban ghetto. They saw the new immigrants as "not quite White." To adjust for this belief, the anthropologist William V. Ripley publishes *The Races of Europe,* and separates "Whites" into a distinct hierarchy of subraces and sub-subraces. (Some become naturalized, organized, voted, and eventually assimilated into "Whiteness." This occurred after WWII as they moved into government-subsidized White suburbs and up the economic ladder.) (In the census of 2010, they are still trying to figure out how become who are not fully "White" or "Black" should be accounted for, it's so absurd, it's laughable! Not really, it's tragic! -- ignorance personified in 2010 America!)

1922-
Who is White becomes a question for the courts; so when the 1790 Naturalization Act restricted naturalized American citi-

zenship to Whites only in the early 20th Century, new arrivals petition the courts to be legally designated White to qualify for citizenship. The Supreme Court concluded that Japanese were not legally White because science classified them as Mongoloid (Yellow) rather than Caucasian (White). The court then contradicted itself by concluding that Asian Indians were not legally White, (although they were classified as Caucasians). The courts got really ridiculous and declared that "Whiteness" is based on "the common understanding of the White man."

1924-
The declaration of who are Black changes.

In 1866, the rule is that "every person having one-fourth or more Negro blood shall be deemed a colored person." The percentage changes in 1910 to 1/16th and then in 1924, the Virginia Racial Purity Act defines Black persons as having any trace of African ancestry or the prevailing "one-drop" rule. Since most people cannot prove their ancestry and the rule is applied subjectively.

1977-
In 1974 the Equal Educational Opportunity Act, the federal Office of Management and Budget Issues Directive 15 forced the government to create a standard government definition of race and ethnicity. The categories turned out to be arbitrary, inconsistent, and exposed how different groups are defined. "Black" was defined as a "race" but "White" was not. "Hispanic" is identified as a pattern of colonization and excludes non-Spanish parts of Central and South America. The "American Indian or Alaskan Native" must be supported with "cultural identification through tribal affiliation or community recognition." Categories were amended in 1996, and a new one, "Native Hawaiian and Other Pacific Islander," was added to the "absurd list."

2000-
<u>Credited with inventing "race":</u>

1. Carolus Linnaeus (1707-1778)
2. Johann Blumenback (1752-1840)
3. Arthur de Gobineau (1816-1882)

<u>What I believe:</u>

Racism was invented during the time that tens of thousands of Africans were captured, enslaved and transported in chains to the Americas to work as field hands and manual workers for European owners.

If I know this, what do the scientists and professors at Harvard and the other universities know? What do the great doctors of this age know?

What do you believe?

Lesson #1

Facts to be Verified by Individual Investigation

After completing Lesson #1, you should be on your way to investigate the following truth for yourself:

1. "Race" is not biological; it is a social construct made in America to justify slavery.

2. Race as separate biological groups cannot be scientifically verified; there is no "race" gene.

3. Scientists do not consider "race" as a fact.

4. There is only one human group, "homo sapiens sapiens"

5. According to current scientific findings, modern man originated in Africa and groups migrated to other areas on earth.

6. Human variation is only skin deep or due to social, cultural or environmental differences/causes.

7. Races have been defined differently at different times in the history of America.

8. Is there any belief(s) you would have to give up if there is only one race?

9. How would you change if you were no longer "White" or "Black"?

10. Are you a "racist" – are you Black or White or Human?

Let's proceed to Lesson #2- Race Based Superiority

Letter #2 – What is the Benefit of Having "Races?"

Dear Reader,

At this point, we will be covering the period in history where we find America divided into "free" and "enslaved." The men in charge of the development of this country were having problems with declaring this a country with great emphasis on equality and the rights of man while at the same time engaging in "bondage."

At first it was easy because "indentured servants" could be anyone and their status was based on the "debt" that they were overcoming. When people from Africa came into the picture, religion was brought into the mix. Since Africans were for the most part if not exclusively, not Christians, they could be demonized if they did not choose to become "Christians." Many African slaves immediately used that "loophole" to obtain their status as a "human being" worthy of freedom. (That loophole was immediately closed when the African slaves took advantage of this and converted to Christianity in such abundance!)

Then a conscious decision was made to give preference to one group. It is at this point that the status of "superiority" was given to the White race; and the status of "inferiority" was given to the Black race. There was also created a middle group, which has been called different things, "Brown," "Mixed," or "Mullatto."

Fast forward to my lifetime, this is an incident involving my Father that shows how well the system that was started during slavery prevails in practice and in power to today. My Father ("Papa") was taken to the emergency room on the weekend and after the initial examination by a White doctor he decided that Papa needed to be seen by a specialist who was not available on the weekend. The doctor got on the phone with the specialist he was trying to persuade to come to the hospital. The doctor says, "He (referring to Papa) is "mullatto." The specialist came and saved my Papa's life!

In this lesson we will cover how and when this system of "privilege" was developed and how it still affects our lives if we are shown how to "see."

I am so happy to have you on this journey as we re-visit our past …

Ms. Johnnie

Lesson #2

Race Based Superiority Established

If you are White, you are right!
If you are Brown, stick around!
If you are Black, get back!

Abraham Lincoln, the sixteenth President of these United States of America says it well regarding the designation of "superiority" for one of the races. He makes his desires and intentions quite clear in the following statements:

> Abraham Lincoln says:
>
> I am not, nor ever have been in favor of bringing about in any way the social and political equality of the White and Black races – that I am nor ever have been in favor of making voters or jurors out of Negroes, nor of qualifying them to hold office, nor to intermarry with White people; and I will say in addition to this that there is a physical difference between the White and Black races which I believe will forever forbid the two races living together on terms of social and political equality. And inasmuch as they cannot live, while they do remain together, there must be the position of superior and inferior, I am as much as any other man in favor of having the superior position assigned to the White race.
>
> I have no purpose to introduce political and social equality between the White and Black races. There is a physical difference between the two, which, in my judgment, will probably forever forbid their living together upon the footing of perfect equality; and inasmuch as it becomes a necessity that there must be a difference, I, as well as Judge Douglas, am in favor of the race to which I belong having the superior position, I have never said anything to the contrary.

Over two-hundred years later a White man begs his fellow White members to get over it, to give up their status of "superiority!"

Andrew M. Manis, a White man, on YouTube in 2009, wonders:

When Are WE Going to Get Over It?

How long before we White people realize we can't make our nation, much less the whole world, look like us? How long until we White people can –once and for all- get over this hell-conceived preoccupation with skin color? How long until we White people get over the demonic conviction that White skin makes us superior?

Dividing the slaveholders and the enslaved into "races" might not look like such a big deal but it's the meaning that went with the "differences." Why then you might ask why was the color of skin or the shape and texture of head and hair so important that people would fight, maim and kill over those differences. What was it about being White; you might wonder what infused White people in the past with such beliefs?

While race does not reside in nature, it dominates politics, economics and culture. Let's trace how our social institutions "make" race real by disproportionately channeling resources, power, status and wealth to White people often in ways we do not notice or acknowledge. It seems "natural" and we all take it for granted.

In this lesson you will learn how it all started. Understanding the history will help us to understand what we have got to do now to save ourselves.

This lesson will explore the powerful beginning of "racism" that still grips America and threatens the future of us all.

The following facts are offered as we trace the race myth to the next phase in the American history (from Race-The Power of an Illusion: 3-Part documentary about race in society, science & history, www.pbs.org/race):

1. *While the concept of Race is man-made it doesn't stop people from believing that it is scientific/ biological, "racism" is true.* Race became a powerful social idea that gives people different access to opportunities and resources. Our country has turned a myth into a hoax that benefited White people. (The law of diminishing returns has kicked in and now this belief in "races" is destroying our country, whatever you call yourself, "Black" or "White."

2. *The notion of "Colorblindness" will not end racism.* People are going to accept the truth about the concept of race and then decide to "restart education" with equal chances for learning that can make this nation "smart" again, based on "teaching and learning" not assigned "superiority" measured and proven by a "bell-curve testing standards."

3. *Slavery came first, then race.* Because all American slaves had a similarity of "skin color" which meant they could be easily identified and associated with slavery and "inferiority" this system became very successful even after a century and a half after slavery ended.

4. *The White Race and freedom became a "natural" pairing like the pairing of the Black race and servitude.* While America was founded on "All men are created equal," the economy was based on slavery. The creation of the concept of race "justified" the enslavement of some and the privileges of others.

5. *Race became the justification for slavery and inequalities as nature-made.* The concept of race served a purpose that served the White race very well and wrecked havoc to the lives of the Black race. White superiority became as natural as breathing and Black inferiority became just as natural. While it justified slavery, it also justified the extermination of Indians, exclusion of Asian immigrants, and the taking of Mexican lands, while hypocritically proclaiming to be a fair and just country. "Racism" became an institutionalized part of American's government, laws, and society and exist alive and well in the education system!

Timeline:

1680-
Slavery became permanent and heritable for "Negroes." Black people were treated worse in every aspect of life. If you were White you were always considered superior and deserved benefits for that and that alone. Slavery as an institution grew bigger and bigger and the "differences" between the two races grew as well.

1705-
During this period the distinction between freed or slave Black did not matter and whether you were a rich White or a destitute White you were considered privileged and superior. Psychologically Whites identified with rich Whites while Blackness became synonymous with slavery and inferiority.

1776-
Freedom comes with a differentiation in "Black" or "White."

The words that Thomas Jefferson put in the Declaration of Independence about the equality and natural rights of man only applied to Whites. While that document laid the foundation for a great American democracy, it from its inception stopped America from ever being a great country until it deals with the "lie," the "hoax" that now fails America and dooms America to "inferiority and ignorance for all" in the new global society. This was the time when the line was drawn in the sand: America would choose to build its success on a "hoax" by justifying slavery with the "inferior nature" of slaves. This is when the concept was put in stone that substantiated the belief in racial difference and White supremacy.

1781-
The founding father Thomas Jefferson is the one who proposes the theory of "innate Black inferiority."

With Notes on the State of Virginia, Jefferson becomes the first prominent American to suggest innate Black inferiority: "I advance it therefore, as a suspicion only, that Blacks... are inferior to the Whites in the endowments of body and mind." It is Thomas Jefferson who developed the plan to "rationalize slavery" by calling on an emerging **"science"** to provide the "proof."

"Racism" is as natural in America as apple pie. To hear a Black or White person say that they are not "racist" makes me cringe from lack of truth and awareness. Whites believe it to the core and see all of the evidences that demonstrate "proof." Blacks really and truly believe that they are inferior and are ashamed of the "evidences" that prove the point. The really sad, and tragic fact is that because they cannot see the presence of some forms of racism right before their very eyes, or understand their own involvement in its continuation they "really believe" that they are not "racist" or "prejudiced."

While the designation of "White superiority" and "Black inferiority" was decided and designated at that point in America before the ending of slavery, it continued, and was enforced after the ending of slavery following the Civil War. Keeping this differentiation became the obsession of this Nation.

It is not the purpose of this book to re-hash or go into the history of this discrimination and social engineering to enforce the superiority of one group and the inferiority of the other.

For those of you, who are unaware, do not believe this happened, or want to refresh your memories, you must pursue the history of the period between the end of the Civil War to today.

As a "Black" person, I have always been keenly aware of this oppression of one group for the benefit of the other, even now a great sadness comes over me as to what happened in my beloved country.

This is when as an African American, the notion that if you are White you are right, if you are Brown, stick around; and if you are Black, get back, was very real in my life! I recently came across these words in the song of the blues that puts the sentiment to music:

Me and a man was workin' side by side

> Here is what it meant:
> They were payin' him a dollar an hour
> They was payin' me fifty cents
> Sayin': If you're white, you're right
> If you're brown, stick aroun'
> But as you black, oh brother,
> Get back, get back, get back.

To keep the "races" pure, marriages between the races were not allowed and for individuals with one drop of Black blood, earned the classification of Black. This kept the differentiation of races very simple and easy to enforce.

As simply put, America was founded by men who believed that people of color were inherently inferior to Whites. They created a collective consciousness, from which institutions were born, that reflected their racial views: Schools, courts, legislative bodies, businesses, the arts and sports, as well as churches.

Most White Americans tend to equate racism with the activities of the Ku Klux Klan, the Skinheads or neo-Nazis who direct acts of violence at people of color. They don't realize that the disease manifests itself in more subtle ways, in the form of an attitude that triggers behavior they deem "natural."

The beliefs and actions of many Whites today reflect a prejudice that they may not be conscious of. They have been programmed to feel and behave in a certain way in regards to Blacks. Their inherent and subconscious feeling of superiority toward Blacks kicks in automatically.

The pollution of racism blankets the entire nation, and the reason most White people don't see it is that they are the pollutant-carriers and producers – and they don't even know it, or don't want to believe that they are. I don't blame them because they have never been told the truth.

Now that you are getting the facts and the effects of the facts on your lifestyle and your future, you are in a position to make a positive difference! Accepting the facts is going to be very difficult and this is how I would explain it:

If I as a Black person put $10 in a bank and a White person puts in the same amount at that bank and after I write a check for $5 I get a notice of bounced checks and insufficient funds; while the White person writes unlimited amounts of checks and everything is fine, while they put in the same $10, they write up to $100 checks and they get a notice from the bank encouraging them to write more checks. It is going to be very difficult for me to convince the White person that there is something wrong with that bank. (Blacks and Whites face a different reality in this country and Whites either don't know it or are in "conscious denial.")

In the beginning

Thomas Jefferson once stated that "it is certain that Blacks and Whites can never live in a state of equal freedom under the same Government, so insurmountable are the barriers which nature, habit, and opinion have established between them."

Alexis de Tocqueville voiced this perspective too, observing in **Democracy in America.** That while he did not believe "that the White and Black races will ever live in any country upon equal footing," he anticipated "the difficulty to be still greater in the United States than elsewhere."

He predicted that the lingering consequences of slavery would forever poison race relations here. "Slavery recedes," he maintained, "but the prejudice to which it has given birth is immovable."

More on the "The World Before Racism" – for those of you who would like to do further research. A Dr. Lisa Farrington, an art historian, curator, author, educator and 2007-2008 Cosby Endowed Professor in Humanities at Spelman College gave a lecture on November 8, 2007 that covered:

When did racism begin?

Has the well-worn antagonism between Black and White always existed in some form or another? Have Africans and their progeny in the Diaspora always been at odds with, or victimized by, western cultural forces? Or is this dichotomy a relatively new phenomenon? Conventional historical texts don't readily address this subject. Or they avoid it, for example, by glossing over Moorish (African Muslim) supremacy in Southern Europe, which lasted some 800 years, by terming the period the "Dark Ages," and by focusing on the activities of Northern Europe during this time.

While it is possible to write and rewrite history with each new age and its sociopolitical hegemony- that is, to put a spin on historic events so as to portray westerners in the most flattering light-it is not so simple a matter to alter history when you use primary source documents as your touchstones, such as original writings and works of fine art and architecture.

These documents have not been historically altered; and they offer a very different history of Africans in the West than the one most of us have access to. Such documents tell us that the ancient world was without race hatred; that the Greeks believed Africans to be their betters; that the Medieval Catholic popes looked to African Christians for aid and financial rescue during the crusades, that 10th and 11th century Germans glorified an African saint above all others. To know true history, one must examine the art works and documents produced during each age-which are the truest expression of a culture, untainted and unfiltered by modern prejudices...

South Carolina Senator James Henry Hammond ruminated in 1861:

In all social systems there must be a class to do the menial duties, to perform the drudgery of life. That is, a class requiring but a low order of intellect and but little skill. Its requisites are vigor, docility, fidelity. Such a class you must have, or you would not have that other class which leads progress, civilization, and refinement. It constitutes the very mudsill of society and of political government... Fortunately for the South, she has found a race adapted to that purpose at her hand. A race <u>inferior</u> to our own, but eminently qualified in temper, in vigor, in docility, in capacity to stand the climate, to answer all her purposes. We use them for our purpose, and we call them slaves."

John Hope Franklin believed that White Americans must accept slavery's impact on race relations today. "White Americans can't say, 'Well, it was my great-granddaddy who had slaves.' They are the direct beneficiaries even today of the opportunities and greed that existed in the 18th and 19th centuries. They need to see the connection between slavery and their privilege today," he said.

Black people are the magical faces at the bottom of society's well. Even the poorest Whites, those who must live their lives only a few levels above, gain their self-esteem by gazing down on us. Surely, they must know that their deliverance depends on letting down their ropes. Only by working together is escape possible. Over time, many reach out, but most simply watch, mesmerized into maintaining their unspoken commitment to keeping us where we are, at whatever cost to them or us. -Derrick Hill

And from this point on in every way the powers of government and society have tried everything legal and not legal to keep the deemed inferior race in poverty. Although poverty afflicts members of all the "races" its victims tend to be largely people of color. Prejudice and discrimination have created a disparity in the standards of living, providing some with excessive economic advantage while denying others the bare necessities for leading healthy and dignified lives. Poor housing, deficient diets, inadequate health care, insufficient education are consequences of poverty that afflict Blacks, American Indians, and Hispanic Americans more than they afflict the rest of the population. The cost to society at large is heavy.

The evil consequences of slavery are still visible in America. They continue to affect the behavior of both Black and White Americans and prevent the healing of old wounds.

The Precepts of American Slavery Jurisprudence

1. Inferiority – superiority of Whites, inferiority of Blacks

2. Property is the status of the inferior group

3. Powerlessness: keep Blacks as powerless as possible so that they will be submissive and dependent in every respect, not only to the master but to Whites in general; and limit accessibility to redress

4. Racial "purity" a drop of any blood other than White makes one not White

5. Family: Recognize no rights of the Black family, destroy the unity of the Black family, demean and degrade Black women, Black men, Black parents, and Black children; and then condemn them for their conduct and state of mind

6. Education and Culture: Deny Blacks an education, deny them knowledge of their culture, and make it a crime to teach Blacks how to read or write

7. Religion: use religion to condition, submission to your master

8. Liberty –Resistance: limit Blacks' opportunity to resist, bear arms, rebel or flee, curtail their freedom of movement, freedom of association, and freedom of expression

9. By any means Possible: Support all measures, including the use of violence, that maximize the profitability of slavery and that legitimize racism. Oppose, by the use of violence if necessary, all measures that advocate the abolition of slavery or the diminution of White supremacy.

But the truth was that our nation was founded explicitly, prospered implicitly, and still often lives uneasily on the precept of Black inferiority and White superiority. …that percept helped to legitimize slavery in America and served to justify the segregation of African Americans in this nation. To this day, the premise of Black inferiority and White superiority remains an essential element of the "American identity," mesmerized as we still are by race and color. – A. Leon Higginbotham, Jr.

Conditioning that can last and last and last …

… the precepts pertaining to inferiority and powerlessness continue to haunt America even today, although it is now more than one hundred and forty years after the Thirteenth Amendment abolished slavery.

Lesson #2

Facts to be Verified by Individual Investigation

1. Trace the history of White Supremacy using the state of South Carolina

2. Trace the difference between education, health care and economic opportunity for White and Blacks in the state

3. Compare the relationship between poverty, illiteracy and race

4. How was submission used as a method to support White supremacy?

5. Cite some major ways Blacks used to cope with White supremacy

6. Trace Uncle Tomism-striving to identify actively with White Carolina and its value

7. How do you define "Blacks" and "Whites?"

8. Are Blacks "inferior" to "White?"

9. Are Whites "superior" to "Blacks?"

10. How do you define a "racist?"

Letter # 3 – Let's Get Off the Curve!

Dear Readers,

Have you ever heard, "What you don't know can't hurt you?"

Well, I'm here to tell you that, "What you don't know can hurt you, and hurt you very badly!"

In Lesson #1 we covered the origin of the concept of "race" in the American society. The concept took hold and became a "scientific fact" that became the law of the land. Then in Lesson #2 we covered how and when the difference between the two races, Black and White was assigned different positions. Whites were given the preferential, "superior" status and Blacks were given the "inferior" position.

It was at that time that two Americas were established. The experiences of a Black person are completely different from the experiences of a White person. I am "fortunate" to have been born when the lines were very distinct so I can share my experiences to help us as we navigate an America where the "physical and visible" signs have been removed but still enforced through "invisible and mental" methods. We must find out where the "mines" are buried so we can hopefully de-fuse them and save the future of America!

Having been born and lived in this country as a Black person for over a half century I see a Black America and a White America! White people have the "power" and the wealth so they have their "right" to think or not to think about Black people and if they decide to think about us they have the right to think whatever they wish at any time and change at any time. As a Black person I have to think about White people at all times, under all circumstances because what they think, how they think, when they think affects my "survival" and "safety/security" at ALL times!

In this lesson on the "bell curve" I have to pray that I will be able to clearly state the case that until we remove the "curve" out of our educational system, America's educational system is going to get worse and worst even worst than where we are today!

The "bell curve" is perfectly effective as a mechanism of "institutionalized race-ism" and equally effective in "anchoring" our educational achievement to the bottom of the Global Society as the "how many feathers on a chicken" kept Blacks from qualifying to vote before the Civil Rights Movement!

America is located on a "minefield of race-ism" that has locked America out of the educational competition that the rest of the Global Society is successfully engaging!

The "normal bell curve" standard must be removed! We must pray that the "scholars" of this century will lead us to an "absolute system" where standards are set whether White students meet them or not, designating preference is failing American education and consequently America (and the World)! Mediocrity lives and breeds in a "bell curve" system! - Ms. Johnnie

SECTION 2
INSTITUTIONALIZATION
OF THE MYTH

Lesson # 3

The Bell Curve Tale
"Standardized Race-ism"

Lessons from Einstein:

"Any intelligent fool can make things bigger, more complex. It takes a touch of genius, and a lot of courage to move in the opposite direction." We have to simplify, simplify, simplify. It takes more time, more thought, and more courage upfront to develop simple, straightforward systems and processes. But the payoffs at the end are enormous. So why do we feel the need to "customize" our systems and processes? Best practice approaches can bring greater competitive advantage through simplicity and efficiency.

"Insanity, doing the same thing over and over and expecting different results." Change is hard. But continuing as we have always done is a sure path to failure, and certainly failure is even harder! If the process isn't working, then change it. If the system isn't supporting the business, then swap it out. If the people don't have the right skills,

> then train them or replace them. Of course, you probably won't be able to do it all at once, incremental change is more easily implemented, less disruptive and often more effective.

I attended the Black school system where the standard was 100%. That means that if you have 50 items on a test, each item has a value of 2-points. If you get 50 items correct then you have a score of 100%. If the highest score on a given test is 25 items, that means that the score is "50" and that is bad, a "failing" score.

On a bell curve standard, 50 could become the 99th percentile and all the remaining scores will fall along the "normal bell curve." If you see how bad that is, then it gets worse, if the "highest" score consistently falls below 50, the College Board in the case of the SAT will "recalibrate" the normal bell curve and make the lower score the 99th percentile.

I am not going to even try to explain exactly how the testing world is using the bell curve system but I will try my best to get you interested in "making" the testing business open up and let us know how the bell curve standard works and why we would want to keep it.

In a bell curve system the tested must give a "race" and how do they use "race" to score the test? In the beginning the races were "White," "Black," and "Asian." What "racial" options do they have now?

How are they able to come up with a "racial" grouping of scores? How does the one drop un-White blood rule apply?

Why can't we have a testing standard where "race" is not a factor? Why can't we have a score that reflects the "percentage" of the number of items the tested answers correctly?

If all students answer less than 50% of the test correctly, we would have 100% failure in an absolute system. We would get an accurate picture of how students are doing! Likewise we could aspire to 100% of our students obtaining 100% scores.

When you put the scores into the normal bell curve standards, how students are doing is distorted and everyone gets a false impression that "some" students are doing well. When America was only dealing with Americans, this system worked, and it worked especially well in a race-based society where "White" is superior and "Black" is inferior.

Let me try to present the case against the "bell curve system" another way. The highest score on the SAT today is 2400. I would think that even on this system, a score of at least 90% would be necessary to be considered anything to rave about. Well, there is a high school in the city where I live that is considered #12 in the country by the U.S. News Report and the average score of that school is approximately 1800 (71% of 2400)! Does anybody get it?

There are two things that I would like to bring up at this time and of course, I have this perspective because I have a "Black" perspective.

In the "Black" school system before Brown vs. the Board of Education. If "100" is the standard then that's the standard. Everybody has the opportunity to score from 0-100. Everybody has the possibility of making a 100 or any number from 0-100. If everybody fails, everybody fails and it's back to the "teaching mode" until students pass.

On a bell curve system, something wonderful is made of whatever the score is. There is no incentive to study hard and the test's norm guarantees the "White race" advantage. The items on the test can never be taught because it would skew the test that measures "innate" capabilities.

The testing companies don't even do the "normal bell curve" statistics correctly! In a true bell curve system, no one is ever capable of having a perfect score. So when I see in the newspaper a picture of a student who got a perfect score, I cringe, because I realize that "mediocrity" has consumed the bedrock of our educational system.

Like I have said, I find that my "Black" world is completely different from the "White" world. In my world, "the glass is half full is the same as the glass is half empty, you still need another half to get to full." If saying it's half full is going to make you feel better and stop there then that is really bad. If saying the glass is half empty and that motivates you to get the other half which is a good thing! To be satisfied and hold on to a half glass is not good!

The scores on our national tests are telling us that we are doing very well because our bell curve standard will never let us see otherwise. This however puts us at #31 in the Global Society!

This is when our "delusion of grandeur" kicks in and makes us incapable of accepting where we are, what we have to do to get better, and then let the "teaching and learning" begin for every student!

This might be good time to bring in a statement that the new Secretary of Education recently said on Face the Nation: "Our 15 year olds are # 31 compared to the rest of the World, but our educational system is #1 in the World!

Time for an exorcism!!!

America is in denial.

A country that is still scoring national tests based on "race" is using an antiquated system. If there is only one race, the human race, basing your educational system on a "race-based" standard is very similar to the "how many feathers on a chicken" test that was given to "certify" citizens to vote when you were trying to have a "fair" system to assure the registration of Whites and the disenfranchisement of Blacks.

What I call "corporate greed" has put a nail in the coffin of the educational system in America. The officers at the College Board and the Educational Testing Service are so busy receiving their outrageous salaries that they haven't given much thought to anything but loving their jobs!

This is where "race-ism" comes into the picture. Because the curve gives America the "racial difference" (or gap) that assures everybody that Whites are still superior and Blacks are still inferior there is no care or concern. (Like trying to get people to understand that there is a problem with "the bank" when they get ample returns on their deposits; it's going to be hard to get those same people to "see" that there is a problem with the "testing" system)

The "bell curve standards" have to be removed before this country will have a chance of moving forward in the area of education. Education is the key and the bell curve standards assure superior status to Whites but at a price and the price has carried us from being number one in the world to number thirty-one (31st is the latest according to Secretary of Education Arne Duncan) and still falling. The economic meltdown confirms that the lack of education in our country affects our economic standards just like it was in 1983, in *A Nation at Risk*.

While I was not the best student in college or graduate school, I learned what I needed to know in statistics at Spelman College to raise the right questions at this point in history to help my country see that we have to restart education in America. I can be smart when I want to (motivated) and study hard enough to get the grade I want. At the University of South Carolina there was a professor who taught Tests & Measurements and had the reputation that no Black person could pass his class. Well, that motivated me, so of course I enrolled in his class and

I got one of the few A's that I got in college or graduate school! So please trust me, call in Michael Moore to pick up the people at College Board and Educational Testing Service (ETS) and ask them a few questions about how they "score" their tests.

Now this is the hardest task facing me. In this chapter, I am going up against Harvard University and the rest of the intellectual world. Is this where the David and Goliath story comes in? I hope you know by now that I like challenges and I will take on the odds!

This is what I believe could possibly be the motive behind the no one questions the "bell curve" standards. I believe the academic world bought into the race myth and the superiority hoax so well that they loved the "bell curve" because it is statistics (scientific) and it proves that race and superiority is not biased, it's substantiated by "science."

Well, what can I say other than let's look at it through my "eyes." It really scared me when a professor at Harvard wrote a book, (**Bell Curve**) I knew then that things were getting really bad, "ignorance" and "arrogance" had come together for a "perfect storm!"

I knew I had to try to do something to shine a light into darkness. In 1995 I wrote a "Letter to the Editor" and sent it to *Black Issues in Higher Education* and the *Chronicle of Higher Education*. *Black Issues in Higher Education* chose to print it and the *Chronicle of Higher Education* chose not to print it. The letter appeared in the January 12, 1995 issue of *Black Issues in Higher Education* and it is presented below for your consideration:

A Bell Tale

Dear Editor:

Please ask your readers to help me solve this mystery. How can a professor from Harvard University named Richard J. Herrnstein and Charles Murray be so mis-educated and have the audacity to call his book, "The Bell Curve," non-fiction, and not be challenged by Black academia?

Doesn't Dr. Herrnstein know that the "normal bell curve theory" is similar to "The Three Little Pigs," Cinderella" and "Alice in Wonderland," and goes like this:

Once upon a time, in the 17th and 18th centuries, mathematicians were asked by gamblers to develop principles that would improve the chances of winning at cards and dice. A mathematician by the name of DeMoivre in the 1730s developed the equation for the first "normal curve."

Educators and psychologists began using the normal bell curve theory, by then making a "fairy" assumption. They assumed that certain "human" traits were distributed along the theory of the "normal bell curve" as other random things might. One of those traits was later named "intelligence" (which really isn't a human trait, because, according to my [former] psychology professor at Spelman College... the only definition of intelligence is an operational definition – intelligence is whatever an intelligence test measures).

Well, the next thing you know, IQ becomes the great crystal ball in the hands of educators. And like long ago, when only White people could correctly give the number of feathers on a chicken to "qualify" to vote, the standardized, norm-based tests are used to "qualify" our students in today's schools in the South.

But, thank goodness, the IQ tale and the demonic powers of probability or self-fulfilling prophesies (strategic tracking) didn't reach the little Town of Mitchelville (now Hilton Head Island) where my ancestors, in 1863, were preparing to enter the country as freedmen. They didn't know anything about the normal bell curve. Maybe they were too absorbed into finding out why they didn't get their forty acres and a mule. Anyway, they bought into a Yankee idea that education might be our only saving grace – with an education everybody can be smart!

We did very well with the idea until a movement called desegregation came along which put us into mainstream schools [where] we were rudely introduced to the normal bell curve story. Well, life hasn't been the same. The people who still relied on education for their salvation were…blocked at the classroom door by a "percentile" gatekeeper.

And now we come back to 1994, where we meet Richard J. Herrnstein and Charles Murray and we assume that when the gods were passing out IQs, they started from the East, and gave most of it out in Asia, then gave the rest to Europe; then they looked into their pockets and found a few left over so they sprinkled those over Africa and the rest is his-story…The beginning of The End.

This normal bell curve theory is wreaking havoc in our great country. In 1983 we got a wake-up call, but it was too loud for us so we decided to go back to the original tale for comfort and solace. My fellow humans, its teaching and learning – good old time education – that can save us all, like in the old prayer, "without the loss of one."
I am sorry to say this, but unfortunately it is true: education shut down after desegregation. We offer gifted and talented activities for Whites (based on the "curve"); boring, disrespectful activities for the average; and "special education" for those on the other end of the "curve" (mostly Black). So this country ends up with "A Nation at Risk" and genetics gets the credit or the blame according to good Herrnstein and Murray, and the Whites get rewarded, not on merit (real education which consists of teaching and learning) but on perceived ability gleaned from the "curve."

Somebody, anybody, please help me. I need help to restart education in America. I shudder to think where I would be today if I had gone to schools that dispensed the mis-education that was given to Richard J. Hernstein and Charles Murray. Please let me hear from you. It is illegal, immoral and detrimental to America to permit the systematic discrimination based on the normal bell curve "tale." Stupid is as stupid does, people. Please help me save our children from the no-education schools of post-desegregation.

Johnnie Mitchell

Now this is where "institutionalized" racism is just as powerful today as it was when Blacks were struggling for the right to vote.

I don't know this for sure. I won't be until Michael Moore cleans house at College Board or ETS. I will always be very suspicious about how the bell curve system is used until they are disproven. I really think it's about as fair and "standardized" as the system that was put in place to keep Blacks from qualifying to vote before the Civil Rights Movement.

Many ways were developed to "legitimately" deny Blacks the right to vote. You are probably familiar with many of them like:

- Poll tax: (Black people couldn't afford to pay a tax when they needed every cent to survive; paying a poll tax was a luxury most sharecroppers could not afford)

- Grandfather clause: you could vote only if your grandfather voted (well if your grandfather was a slave who you didn't even know in most cases, this would eliminate about 100% of ex-slaves)

- How many bubbles in a bar of soap (Blacks just couldn't get it right)

- How many feathers on a chicken (only Whites seem to be able to get it right)

How many feathers on a chicken is my favorite and I'll use this one to show how I compare it to what's happening with "bell curve standardized testing system" today.

When a Black person came up to the clerk, he would be asked how many feathers are on the chicken. White people always gave the "right" answer. Black people always gave the "wrong" answer. If anyone tried to fight it, the defense would be that the "test" was equal and fair; and just because only White people got it right it just means they are smarter. Well, the Whites always got it right because the examiner knew the "race" of the person applying and gave it the White "score." When the Black person applied they were assigned the Black "score." It was "consistent," "reliable" and met all of the "normative" requirements.

What I would like to know is how do College Board, the Educational Testing Service and other "standardized tests companies" use "race" in light of the fact that we now have so many different "ethnic" groups in America. Do they allow a student to declare multiple "races?" How do they calculate those? How would they score the test if no "race" for the tester was provided?

I can hardly wait to hear their answers!

The Key Issues to be shared and learned in this **Lesson on the Bell Curve Tale** are the following:

1. Understanding how a "curve" standard keeps you from ever reaching excellence. In an absolute standard system, the test with 20 items would be based on an absolute standard of "100" where each item would have a value of 5. So if you want absolute "excellence" only 100 on the test would be acceptable or 90% or 80%. Now in a "curve" system if the highest score on the test is "60", that becomes the standard or the (100) and the rest of the scores are put on a statistical bell curve.

2. The second key issue is the fact that the "race" of each tester must be known because this is where you have the "hocus-pocus" where Asians score the highest (we don't hear much about this fact) Whites (second highest) and Hispanics, Blacks and Native Americans at the bottom end of the curve. Now, if there are no Black or White or Hispanic or Native American "gene" then how come the race must be known, with different norms that always guarantee the testing folks that White superiority and Black inferiority is always consistent, just like when only superior White people could always know the correct number to the how many feathers on a chicken question

3. When the superior Whites scores go lower than the present low, the scoring is just re-calibrated to keep the superior group superior and the standards lowered that I would think at some point we'll have students entering medical school who can hardly read …

This is where I really need you to do some serious research. If you can find out from the people who are responsible for the "standardized testing" in America, what's the deal here? Why isn't the standard an absolute "100" which means if no one passes then the learners have to go back and study some more. Now we just make the "half full glass" serve as a "full glass" and you get to where we are today. Where is a curve system going to get us?

Scientific Racism

So we have entered the realms of scientific racism. This is the conception of intelligence as a fixed, unitary, biological capacity that was a product of the 19th century. The rise of science led to the increase of scientific rationales for race differences based on "pseudoscientific" disciplines of anthropometry and the use of brain size as an index of intelligence.

In the early 20th century, particularly after World War I, the increased importance of education led to the growth of intelligence tests and other timed paper and pencil tests, such as IQ tests widely interpreted as measures of "intelligence" to assign persons in education or jobs.

One face of this era is Richard Herrnstein, a Harvard psychologist

In the 1970s Harvard psychologist Richard Herrnstein argued that social class was and should be largely a function of intelligence.

In 1994 he and Charles Murray came out with *The Bell Curve* which extended that argument to the view that poverty, low income, welfare dependency, unemployment, divorce, illegitimate pregnancy, crime and a lack of "middle class values" were all in large part produced by a lack of intelligence, and that race differences in such conditions were largely explained by race differences in IQ.

At this point I am going to offer another view of the history of "race" that may shed some differences of opinion on the validity of the Harvard professor:

The Roots of Race

1. According to current scientific findings, what is the origin of modern man?

Most scientists have come to accept the evolutionary theory based on DNA evidence: that modern human originated in Africa about 270,000 years ago. Researchers at Yale, Harvard, and the University of Chicago have traced the genetic roots of the human family ... to the existence of an "African Eve." (*Journal of Science*, October 1996)

2. When was mention first made of "races" as separate biological groups?

Human beings have always come in a variety of hues and statures. The ancient Egyptians, Vikings and Chinese, while fighting and conquering in every corner of the globe, never thought that the people they encountered were biologically different. For most of recorded history the idea of "race" did not exist. This idea entered the social and scientific consciousness during the Age of Exploration and the "discovery" of the New World. Before Europeans took to the seas there was no mention of "race."

The habit of sorting the world's people into distinct groups was first introduced by Swedish taxonomist Carolus Linnaeus, who in 1758 declared that the human species was divided into four basic groups. Later, German anatomist and naturalist Johann Friedrich Blumenbach added an additional category and then redefined all five groups based on geography and appearance, with his variety, the "Caucasians," at the top of the hierarchy of worth (based oddly enough upon perceived beauty), and the "Negroid" at the bottom. These doctrines of racial superiority were then used to justify the expansion and colonization of Africa, Asia and the Americas. The Europeans further developed racist thought in order to establish and maintain slavery, especially in the Americas, with the Germans adding the final "refinement" to modern racism by taking it to ridiculous extremes earlier this century; i.e., the Jewish Holocaust.

"[The] roots and growth of [a ranked hierarchy of races] lie in nothing more 'real' than the conquest, dispossession, enforced transportation and economic exploitation of human beings over five centuries that racial categorization and racist social ordering have served to expedite and justify. As part of [this] legacy... millions of people today continue to accept inherited racial categories as fixed in nature" (from *Race*, by Roger Sanjek, professor of anthropology, Queens College)

"Prior to the 16th century, the world was not race-conscious and there was no incentive for it to become so. The ancient world was a small world...and physical differences...were not very marked... Even when the existence of such physical differences was recognized, they had no immediate social connotations ... It was only with the discovery of the New World and the sea routes to Asia that race assumed a social significance. Even the Crusades failed to make Europe race-conscious...Europeans have not been content merely to accept their present social and political dominance as an established fact. Almost from the very first, they have attempted to rationalize... and prove to themselves that their subjugation of other racial groups was natural and inevitable." (From *The Study of Man,* by Ralph Linton, anthropologist)

3. What is "race"?

The origin of the word "race" is unclear. Some trace it to the Latin *radix,* meaning "root" or "stock," and some others trace it to the Italian *razza,* which means "breed" or "lineage." It is used to designate any aggregate of people that can be identified as a group. According to this usage, persons who have a common ancestry or who share common beliefs or values, or any social or cultural traits, are considered a "race."

By its definition the word "race" is divisive. The term attempts to classify subspecies of human beings according to: (1) physical characteristics such as skin color/hair texture, shape of eyes, (2) psychological and behavioral traits are made to associate with these superficial characteristics, and (3) superior or inferior status is attributed to these traits.

4. Do scientists now consider "race" a fact?

Almost all branches of science officially stopped dividing people into "races" in the mid-1930s. Every day since, scientists have been trying to undo racism that has been perpetuated using five centuries-old outdated scientific methods and doctrines. For example, in 1952, anthropologist Ashley Montagu called race ***"man's most dangerous myth."***

The genetic markers that supposedly divide the human species into "races" represent only a minute fraction of our total genetic endowment. No matter how one tries to divide humanity, there are many that do not fit into any one category. This is because extensive migration and intermixing of people has occurred, causing genetic material to pass between widely separated human populations.

"Race has no basic biological reality." (Jonathan Marks, biologist, Yale University)

"Misconceptions about race have led to forms of racism that have caused much social, psychological and physical harm. These misconceptions have their origin in various papers and books that depend heavily on old and outmoded biological concepts of race." (Leonard Lieberman, anthropologist, Central Michigan University)

" ... differentiating species into biologically defined "'races' has proven meaningless and unscientific as a way of explaining variation, whether in intelligence or other traits." (Statement of the American Anthropological Association)

"Vast new data in human biology, prehistory and paleontology...have completely revamped the traditional notions [of race]." (Solomon Katz, anthropologist, University of Pennsylvania)

'Race' is a social construct derived mainly from perceptions conditioned by events of recorded history, and it has no basic biologic reality." (C. Loring Brace, biological anthropologist, Brown University)

"The old biological definitions of race were based on what people looked like, Now that we have better ways of looking at race...we could construct races based on...fingerprints or blood type, and that would be just as legitimate." (Joseph L. Graves Jr., evolutionary biologist, Arizona State University)

"Racism can be viewed solely as a social problem, although at times it has been used by politicians as a purportedly 'scientific' tool. It is an emotional phenomenon best explained in terms of collective psychology. Racial conflict results from long-suppressed resentments and hostilities. The racist responds to social stereotypes, not to be known scientific facts." (from an anthropology textbook by William A. Haviland)

"The concept of race, masking the overwhelming genetic similarity of all peoples and the mosaic patterns of variation that do not correspond to racial divisions, is not only socially dysfunctional but it biologically indefensible as well." (from *Evolutionary Biology*, by D. J. Futuyma).

5. Does science agree with the principle of one oneness of the Human Race?

"We are one species, one people. Every individual on this earth is a member of Homo sapiens, and the geographical variations we see among peoples are simply biological nuances on the basic theme. The often very deep differences between cultures should not be seen as divisions between people. Instead, cultures should be appreciated for what they really are: the ultimate declaration of belonging to the human species." (Richard Leakey, renowned paleontologist)

Dr. Luigi Luca Cavalli-Sforza, a Stanford Medical School scholar and one of the world's leading geneticists, has compiled a definitive atlas (*History and Geography of Human Genes*) of the genetic profiles of over 1,800 population groups around the world. This work is the most comprehensive survey ever compiled of how humans vary hereditarily. In another one of his books, he states:

The difference between races are ... very limited ... [The genes that react to climate are those that influence external features...It is because they are external that [they]strike us so forcibly, and we automatically assume that differences of similar magnitude exist below the surface... This is simply not so: the remainder of our genetic make-up hardly differs at all.

"Since all human beings are of one species and since all populations tend to merge when they exist in contact, group differentiation will be based on cultural behavior and not on genetic differences." (From the *Biology of Race*, by James King)

"We must remember that what unifies us outweighs what makes us different. Skin color and body shape, language and culture, are all that differentiated the peoples scattered across the earth. This variety, which testifies to our ability to accept change, adapt to new environments and evolve new lifestyles, is the best guarantee of a future for the human race...This diversity, like the changing face of the sea or sky, is minute compared with the infinite legacy we human beings possess in common." (from *The Great Human Diasporas*, by Francesco Cavalli-Sforza)

"All members of the species Homo sapiens are related by common ancestral roots...[T]he biological oneness of the human species does not mean genetic uniformity. Genetic variation among members of the same species is a healthy and necessary condition of life. Adaptation, evolution and survival depend on these variations." (Shidan Lotfi, molecular and cellular biologist)

6. Does genetic science prove our biological oneness?

"Skin color may only be skin deep. Surgeons, thankfully, understand this: in organ transplants a Black donor can be a better match for a White patient than another White person might be." (*Discover Magazine*, November 1994)

"We are beginning to get good data at the DNA level," says Yale University geneticist Kenneth Kidd, who has studied minute variations in the genes of people from 42 different population groups around the globe, and who concludes that DNA data supports the concept of our sameness:

Genetically, I am more similar to someone from China or the Amazon Basin than two Africans living in the same village are to each other. This substantiates that there is no such thing biologically as [different races].

7. Does blood have anything to do with our color?

No. The four blood types (A,<B>AB and O are universal and found in all human populations. An Irishman with Type A blood can receive and give blood to a Ugandan of the same blood type. Blood has nothing to do with the transmission of hereditary material, therefore it makes no sense to describe a person's ancestry in terms of blood; i.e., saying that someone has one-fourth Indian blood has no meaning based on fact.

8. How does science explain human variation; i.e., differences in skin color or height?

Anthropologists attribute our superficial physical traits or phenotypes to adaptation to different environments, such as temperature, humidity, proximity to the equator, wind and many other factors. This is what is referred to as *natural selection*. For example, northern Europeans have developed long, narrow noses to warm extremely cold, damp air to their body temperature; whereas the larger, long noses of Middle Easterners and Northern Africans have evolved from moistening the dry air befor it reaches their lungs. Eskimos generally have more rounded and squat bodies as an adaptation to cold climate, so they can retain body heat and the Tutsi of Rwanda are the tallest of human species because they inhabit regions of intense, arid heat and consequently need to dissipate heat more effectively.

Human skin owes its color to the presence of melanin. Its primary functions are to protect the upper layers of the skin from such hazards as radiation, infections and skin cancers. The particular color of a person's skin represents a tradeoff between the hazards of too much vs. too little solar radiation; i.e., skin cancer on the one hand, and rickets and osteomalacia on the other. The genes of our primitive ancestors were programmed to produce dark skin. The group of Africans who later migrated north in Europe, by a flip of the genetic dice, developed a variant gene that gave them slightly lighter skin. The trend continued for generation after generation, eventually producing other fair-skinned people, such as Swedes.

There is little evidence that any visible differences have any practical advantages. These differences have arisen simply because we are a restless, adventurous, hopeful migratory species whose intelligence and quest for survival has allowed us to survive in almost every corner of the globe.

9. Are there population groups that possess superior intelligence?

No Intelligence Quotient (IQ) Tests meant to measure inherited mental capacity are so seriously limited that comparing average IQ's for various "racial" groups is an erroneous practice and is being discounted as an unreliable indication of a person's ability to learn.

"The attempt to measure "racial" differences in intelligence is impossible and therefore worthless." (Jerry Hirsh, behavioral geneticist, Washington University)

10. Public Enemy #1: the people at the Educational Testing Service, College Board

It's amazing how things get mixed up and wreaks havoc in a country's educational system!
This is the perfect time to take a look back at the "history" of the normal bell curve. In most books on statistics you don't find the name "Abraham de Moive." This is how it really started let's meet Abraham de Moivre:

Abraham de Moivre

French-born British mathematician **Abraham de Moivre** (May 26, 1667 – November 27, 1754) is best known for the fundamental formula of complex numbers $(\cos x + i \sin x)_n = \cos nx + i \sin nx$, where $i = \sqrt{-1}$, called *de Moivre's theorem*.
It is the keystone of analytic trigonometry, linking complex numbers with trigonometry. The result can be used to find explicit expressions for the nth roots of unity, that is, complex numbers satisfying the equation $z_n = 1$. De Moivre never explicitly stated it in his work. However, his familiarity with it is clear from a related

---

formula that he discovered in 1722, namely, $\cos \varphi = .(\cos n\varphi + i \sin n\varphi)_{1/n} + .(- .$

De Moivre's chief works were *The Doctrine of Chances*, (1718), a key contribution to the early history of probability, the *Miscellanea Analytica*, (1730), in which he investigated infinite series, and *A Treatise of Annuities on Lives*, (1752), an application of probability to mortality statistics, and the creation of the theory of annuities. This remarkably original work laid the foundations of the mathematics of life insurance.

De Moivre was born in Vitry, near Paris and spent five years at a Protestant academy at Sedan. From 1682 to 1684, he studied logic at Saumur, then entered the College de Harcourt in Paris and took private mathematical lessons with Jacques Ozanam. De Moivre had the misfortune to be a Huguenot (Calvinist) at the time that Roman Catholic France revoked the Edict of Nantes and began persecuting French Protestants.

De Moivre was imprisoned in Paris for a year and when he was released moved to England. He developed a friendship with Newton and Edmund Halley, which helped him to be elected to the Royal Society in 1697. In 1710, he returned the favor as a member of the Royal Society's Commission to review the rival claims of Newton and Leibniz as the inventors of the calculus. Despite helping the Royal Society get the answer it wanted by supporting Newton, de Moivre later sought Leibniz's help in securing a university chair on the continent. However, nothing came of it and any hope of finding a mathematics chair in England was dashed because he was a foreigner.

De Moivre studied Newton's *Principia* and became such an expert on it that in later years, when asked about some point or another in it, Newton would say, "Go to Mr. De Moivre; he knows these things better than I do."

In 1733 de Moivre derived what is now known as the normal distribution as a method for estimating discrete probabilities, in particular those involving the binomial distribution. Later Pierre de Laplace, motivated by observational science, discovered the means of various samples of n measurements are distributed approximately according to the normal curve. From these approximations Laplace was able only to state the high probability of sample means lying within a given range according to the normal distribution. This approximation of the probability of sums of binomial distribution values is now known as the de-Moivre-Laplace limit theorem.

Prior to the discovery of this theorem, probability and statistics were treated as two separate entities. It was the first example of central limit theorems, most

of which were derived by Pafnuty Tchebycheff and his students Andrei Markov and Aleksandr Lyapunov during the period 1880 to 1920. These theorems unified probability and statistics.

One of the most important examples of a continuous probability distribution, the normal distribution is often referred to as, **"The Bell-Shaped Curve,"** the shape of its graph. An extremely wide range of natural phenomena and are accurately described using the curve. The empirical rule of the normal distribution is that 68% of the area lies under the curve within one standard deviation of the center; 95% of the area under the curve lies within two standard deviations of the center; and 99% of the area under the curve lies within three standard deviations of the center. A standard deviation is the square root of the average of the squares of the deviations from the mean in a frequency distribution.

De Moivre's *The Book of Chances* marked the first appearance of the bell-curve, although the origin of the curve is sometimes attributed to Gauss, who did the most important and fundamental work with the normal distribution; so much so that it is sometimes referred to as the Gaussian distribution.

De Moivre remained at the poverty level all his life, reduced to working as a private tutor or as a consultant to gambling or insurance syndicates, and never obtaining a university position. At the end of his life, he eked out a living by solving problems of chance for gamblers as the resident statistician of Slaughter's Coffee House in London. He died blind and disillusioned, with his contributions to mathematics unrecognized. W.W. Rouse Ball wrote of de Moivre's final days:"The Manner of de Moivre's death has a certain interest for psychologists. Shortly before it, he declared that it was necessary for him to sleep some ten minutes or a quarter of an hour longer each day than the preceding one: the day after he had thus reached a total of something over twenty-three hours he slept up to the limit of twenty-four hours, and then died in his sleep."

Normal Distribution

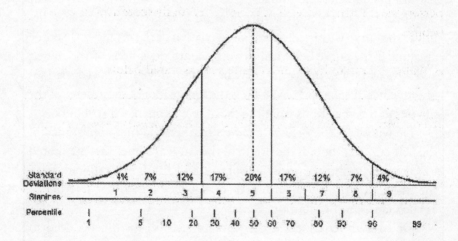

Standard Deviations		4%	7%	12%	17%	20%	17%	12%	7%	4%	
Stanines		1	2	3	4	5	6	7	8	9	
Percentile	1	5	10	20	30	40	50	60	70	80	90	95	99

A bell curve system is not based on "teaching and learning." A statistical principle is inappropriately used as the base of our educational system. Our educational system is inappropriately based on a hocus-pocus/race based probabilities system that keeps our educational system locked into failure!

In an education system where there is an absolute standard, with great teaching and learning a person from any group might have the highest score. In a bell curve system teaching and learning is rather irrelevant and who scores the highest can be controlled.

It means that "teaching and learning" are really bad for a system like this because at the bottom of the theory is that the test is measuring "IQ" or at least innate inheritance and so to teach an inferior Black person the information well, he could eventually score as well as White people.

A Walter Lippman had similar concerns, as stated below:

In the Nov. 15, 1922 issue of The New Republic, Walter Lippman said:

The danger of the intelligence tests is that in a wholesale system of education, the less sophisticated or the more prejudiced will stop when they have classified and forget that their duty is to educate...

Most of the more prominent testers have committed themselves to a dogma which must lead to such abuse. They claim not only that they are really measuring intelligence, but the intelligence is innate, hereditary and predetermined. They believe that they are measuring the capacity of a human being for all time and that this capacity is fatally fixed by the child's heredity.

Intelligence testing in the hands of men who hold this dogma could not but lead to an intellectual caste system in which the task of education had given way to the doctrine of predestination.

...Welcome to the education system in America!

Lesson #3 – Facts to be Verified by Independent Investigation

1. Why is the normal bell curve system used by College Board and Education Testing Service?

2. If there is no scientific way to classify a student according to "race," how is "race" used in the scoring?

3. Why do "Asians" score higher than other "races?"

4. If 2400 is the highest possible score on the SAT, why is 1800 considered so highly that a school can be #12 in the country?

5. How is "intelligence" factored into standardized tests?

6. If a student studies really hard after taking the SAT or any norm-based achievement test, and retakes the test making a very high score, would his score be challenged due to a premise of your test that it taps into "intelligence" therefore variation of test results must conform to standards that can only be broken by "cheating," not "teaching and learning."

7. What is the purpose of "re-calibrating," how is it done, why is it done?

8. What's the "value" of an "absolute-standard?" For example, if 2400 is the goal, then 2400 would be the goal for everyone; everyone is therefore capable of reaching 2400 or not and everybody knows where each tester stands. Is that possible on a bell curve norm-based standards?

9. What would be the difference in a "norm-based standard" and an "absolute standard"?

10. Which system encourages "teaching and learning?"

Letter #4 – The Gains and Losses after Brown vs. the Board of Education

Dear Reader,

This law is one that is probably the BEST thing that has happened to "Black" people and the WORST thing that happened to "Black" people!

Most of us know the good things that this law brought to Black people. In a short time some Black people have been able to make great strides in mainstream America. While it broadened opportunities for some Blacks, it imprisoned a group of Blacks and eliminated the use of education as a means of advancement.

In South Carolina a poor Black student such as me had an opportunity to go to a school where teachers were concerned about my advancement, encouraged me and said that I could be anything I wanted to be if I worked hard enough. In my segregated pre-Brown vs. Board of Education schooling I arrived at Spelman College from probably the poorest area in South Carolina with a better education than students from middle class families in the northern cities who had to take remedial reading and math while I did not.

Then "so-called integration" came to my hometown and I saw Black children's future put in the hands of White people who fought desegregation, took their children out of the public schools, formed private or church schools leaving Blacks by themselves being taught by the Whites who fought desegregation, sent their children to private or church (White only) schools where the new White school system didn't know our history, didn't encourage advancement and presented a new concept that if you are poor, Black, single parented, qualify for free lunch and didn't test well, "you are not ready to learn." The Black college education department that furnished the Black teachers was closed and put on the White college's campus and that was the end of the source of Black teachers.

The NAACP never went back to check to see why Blacks could learn and learn well before they entered the White school system but now they aren't ready to learn, they are not graduating and the rate of graduation decreased yearly. Black schools that had a great history and reputation were now doing so badly that the State threatened taking over those schools. The Civil Rights Movement was dismantled and that's where things are!

I will offer my subjective view of what happened and how it now affects your future and mine!

If I'm successful in convincing you that a group of Black people are getting a free ride because they cannot get an education if they are poor, qualify for free lunch and don't make a certain score on norm-based tests, will you help to restart education? We need all hands on deck to make our country smart and successful again!

Ms. Johnnie

Lesson #4

Brown vs. the Board of Education, 1954
Blacks Legally Enter White America

Up until this period in the history of America, there was a clear difference between the White America and Black America. The lines were clear. Goals and objectives were clear.

Speaking from my own past, I would say that Black America was focused intensely on trying to get a place at the White American table. Blacks pursued education with a passion. This period from the end of the Civil War to the period of Brown vs. the Board of Education I would think that Blacks did themselves proud. They accomplished, they achieved, in spite of all the opposition from their government and the forces of White supremacy that was unrelenting. They learned, they achieved and they fought for "equality!" They wanted the best for themselves and their country!

I personally would compare the history of Blacks after the Thirteenth Amendment giving us our freedom to today in terms of before Brown vs. the Board of Education and after the Brown vs. Board of Education.

My interpretation is that we won a lot, we were now allowed into the American society. On the other hand we have paid for that opportunity with the loss of a half century of progress in the area of education which negatively impacts every aspect of Black America which ultimately negatively affects the entire country.

Before Brown vs. the Board of Education we struggled, we were determined to be "successful" and to contribute to the success of our country.

However, a serious change in the education of Blacks in the South took place as a result of Brown vs. the Board of Education.

Blacks who were on the road to success after freedom were able to really take advantage of the opportunities that opened up as a result of this legislation.

The group that had not found its way, had not learned how to use education for advancement, this legislation in my opinion, put the education and socialization of our most vulnerable young were put in the hands of people who did not know us and had been "conditioned" to think we were "inferior."

This is where we have to revisit history so that we will have the same frame of reference as we address the challenge to restart our education for a non-racial America that will benefit the present generation and the generations to come.

The Situation of Blacks that Led to the passage of Brown vs. the Board of Education

Blacks in the South after being freed were left to pull themselves up by their own "boot strap."

This presented a great problem for the ex-slaves. While slavery is the worst thing that Blacks could ever experience, slavery did provide them their survival needs, food, a place to stay, and full employment. In freedom, those were the key survival needs that Blacks were least prepared to provide for themselves. Not only were they not prepared for their own survival needs, they had to learn in a hostile climate where the former "owners" did not like it that there possession/asset is now a loss and a possible competitor.

> The passion still remains about that loss as expressed to me by a White history teacher:
>
> I was working at a high school with a White history teacher at a predominantly Black rural school.
>
> In a discussion one day with this history teacher who you would think would be over the fact that the South lost the Civil War and Blacks got their freedom. Well, that was not the case with this White teacher who explained his anger about what went down. He felt that slavery was an economic situation and if Blacks had just stayed cool for another hundred years, America would have outgrown the need for slaves and we would have gotten our freedom and Whites would not have been angry with us. We will always have to endure the anger for getting our freedom prematurely...

Things were really bad for Blacks during this period from the end of the Civil War to the fifties.

Right after the Civil War, the brief Reconstruction period allowed Blacks to really show their readiness for freedom. Since they were in many cases in the majority, they were able to get into politics and do very well. That period is now sometimes referred to as "Black Reconstruction" and then of course Whites took back the power through violence and other intimidations and that period is referred to as White Reconstruction.

In the area of education, Blacks were on their own. White children were provided schoolhouses, bus transportation and the new books. Blacks experienced the flip side.

Eventually Thurgood Marshall was able to take the case of "inequality" to the Supreme Court and won. The issue was "equal" resources.

That was not how the law was put into effect. The Black school system was dismantled and the education of Black children was now put into the hands of the White school system.

The White children in most cases in many places were taken out of the public school system and church and private schools sprung up all over the South; so Blacks did not get to go to school with White children. In some districts, testing results were used to keep the "races" separate. Whites and selected Black students were put in good "magnet" schools. ("Magnet" meaning exceptional schools to "attract" White students to attend the public school system; especially assuring White parents that only highly screened Black students would be attending)

Again, Blacks who had good education, good professions could take advantage of all the other opportunities with the opening up of the American society.

Before "integration" Blacks were forced to live in the same Black community. After "integration" the professional Blacks could now move to the suburbs or the "Whites communities."

Blacks who were still just struggling to survive were left in the rural areas or in the urban pocket at the mercy of a school system that didn't know their language, their culture, their history, their aspirations, the "education path" to success was changed.

A Synopsis of the Brown Decision:

After World War II, a number of cases were brought by African American plaintiffs from Delaware, Kansas, South Carolina, and Virginia, which culminated in the historic 1954 Supreme Court decision, *Brown et al v. Board of Education of Topeka et al.* In each of these cases, parents wanted access to equal facilities, curricula, and instructional materials for their children. They shared the widely held belief that education was the key to opportunity and upward mobility for African Americans.

The central question addressed by the Supreme Court was whether or not segregation of children in public schools solely on the basis of race deprives minority children of equal educational opportunities even when all else is equal. The court ruled that not only was such racial segregation harmful but, to separate Black children from others of similar age and qualifications solely because of their race generates a feeling of inferiority as to their status in the community that may affect their hearts and minds in a way unlikely ever to be undone. The courts asserted that the need for Black children to see themselves in a positive reaffirming way was just as important as curriculum, facilities, and other resources.

The *Brown* decision abolished the laws *requiring* segregated schools in 17 states and the laws *permitting* segregated schools in four other states. The Supreme Court did not outlaw *de facto* segregation typically found in cities outside of the South. Following the decision, school desegregation was not uniformly implemented. While many communities in border states began the process almost immediately, the eight states of the Deep South (AL, FL, GA, LA, MS, NC, SC, and VA), where Blacks constituted 22% or more of the population, did not integrate until the mid 1960s, when they were pushed by the courts.

The Dream Deferred: Progress of Desegregation

After being forced to integrate, many communities withdrew support for public schools and established private academies. These schools were primarily targeted at European American parents, and were sometimes supported with public funds. Virginia closed schools in

Arlington, Charlottesville, and Norfolk for most of the 1958-59 school year; Prince Edward County public schools were closed for several years while a White private academy flourished with state-supported tuition (White, 1994)

Integration was achieved mostly by closing schools serving African American students and busing the students to former Whites-only schools. These arrangements were maintained during subsequent decades. Today, however, Orfield, Eaton, and the Harvard Project (1996) note a trend toward resegregation in the public schools. For the first time since 1954, school segregation is actually increasing for Black students. This gradual undoing of integrated public schooling will be difficult to address legislatively because of the role of private schools.

Busing students was never popular among White parents. Today Black parents also express unwillingness to have their children bused, or their neighborhood school closed to achieve racial balance. Many Black parents believe their children are better off in resegregated schools because they no longer believe integrated schools offer any significant academic advantage.

This belief among some Black parents may be because of the resegregation that often occurs *within* schools via course assignments and "ability grouping." A pattern develops in which low-income minority students experience initial learning difficulties in the early grades, then are evaluated as "low-ability" and placed in low-track, remedial, or special education programs. When they get to high school, they are mostly enrolled in vocational and general programs, while Whites are mostly enrolled in academic program. Because of this compounding of disadvantage, "access to learning opportunities is limited beyond what would be expected from being enrolled in either a disadvantaged school or a low-track-class.

Some observers see the persistent segregation of African Americans, whether through private schooling, resistance to busing, or tracking, as a result of African American parents' lack of ability to mobilize power and resources. Decision-making structures in many rural communities limit the influence African American parents (especially those with low incomes) can have on educational decisions affecting their children. They have few avenues by which they can challenge curriculum choices, instructional strategies, or course placement decisions. School officials often dismiss African American students' absence in advanced and college preparatory courses as a normal reflection of students' interests, academic talents, and parents' lack of interest. However, African American parents have long cared deeply about education and so have their children. Billingsley reminds us:

The value African-Americans place on education has always been extraordinarily high. There is a deep historical and cultural belief in the efficacy of education. Blacks have sought education in every conceivable manner and at every level.

Other Factors Affecting Rural African American Students

Besides the ongoing effects of segregation, a number of other factors affect educational outcomes for rural African Americans. National data indicate African American students, as a sub-population, still do not score on par with their European American counterparts. A recent study by Western Interstate Commission for Higher Education (1998) found that students in rural, small-town locations (Southern region states such as AL, AR, DE, FL, GA, KY, LA, MD, MS, OK, SC, TN, TX, VA, and WV) score significantly below students in rural areas nationwide. Rural schools in all states have less money and poorer educational programs than their more wealthy urban neighbors.

The loss of African American educators. In the old segregated school system, Black children attended schools operated mostly by skilled Black educators. These teachers and administrators were better credentialed and more experienced than their White counterparts (Southern Education Reporting Service, 1959). With integration came massive layoffs: 38,000 African Americans in 17 states lost their positions as teachers and administrators between 1954 and 1965. Things haven't been the same since. As recently as the 1995-96 school year, African American teachers comprised on 7.3% of the teaching force in public schools (National Education Association, 1997).

For many African American children, African American teachers represent surrogate parent figures, acting as disciplinarians, counselors, role models, and advocates. According to one study, low-achieving African American students benefit most from relationships with

African American teachers. African American teachers also tend not to rationalize student failure by blaming family or society.

Educators' lack of focus on school factors. Research on effective schools shows that when teachers focus on factors they can control (instructional issues) instead of factors out of their control (such as students' background) students do better in school. Teachers with this focus, regardless of ethnicity, bring a strong sense of personal and professional efficacy to the classroom.

Resistance to school norms. Instead of submitting to the norms of a school establishment many students experience as oppressive, some students reject European American speech patterns and devalue high academic achievement, inadvertently limiting themselves. However, other African American students respond in the opposite way. These high-achieving African American students cite their awareness of racism and prejudice as a reason to excel, thus preparing themselves to fight these evils.

Improving Outcomes: Two Powerful Approaches. First, educators interested in improving outcomes for rural African American students can begin with an *emancipatory pedagogy,* which goes beyond teaching basic skills to engaging students in critical reflection about realities such as social injustice.

In my own experience as an African American student in segregated schools, we were told we would have to be twice as good as Whites, and were prepared to expect racism and bigotry. But we were also taught we could "fight back" by being excellent. Today, the ranks of African American teachers, the traditional orators of that message, have diminished. And some African American teachers no longer see advocacy, role- modeling, and surrogate parenting as parts of their job. It is possible, though, for teachers of any ethnicity to academically empower rural African American students. Achievement data indicate the pressing need to carry the message that excellence is *possible* and *essential* for rural African American students.

Second, educational research indicates that schools can best improve the academic achievement of African American children only when they work in partnership with parents. Forty-four years after the *Brown* decision, educators must join with *African American communities* that have lacked access to resources or power to address together the ongoing educational crisis playing itself out in rural counties, particularly in the South.

Appropriate education for poor children and children of color can only be devised in consultation with adults who share their culture. Black parents, teachers of color, and members of poor communities must be allowed to participate fully in the discussion of what kind of instruction is in their children's best interest.

ERIC ® *Clearinghouse on Rural Education and Small Schools: Rural African Americans and Education: The Legacy of the Brown Decision by Patricia S. Kusimo*

Summary of the Value of the Brown decision in the South

- Today the high school graduation rate for African American is somewhere between 30% and 50%

- The worst thing that could happen to "education" in the South for both Blacks and Whites

- Bringing Black children and White children into the same school system has been a dismal failure for "education" in South Carolina

- The NAACP seemed only concerned about whether Blacks were sitting next to Whites (that never happened either, but they never looked back)

- They never looked back to see the horrors that "so called integration" in schools brought to poor uneducated Blacks

Lesson #5 – Facts to be Verified by Independent Investigation

1. Compare the academic achievement of Blacks before Brown vs. the Board of Education and after the law (Period from the Civil War to Brown and after Brown to the present)

2. Where have all the Black teachers gone in SC?

3. Where do the teachers and administrators send their children to school in SC?

4. Has the NAACP or any civil rights group gone into the schools to see what is happening to Black children, how they are treated, how they are taught or not taught and why poor Black children could learn and achieve in the poorly funded schools before Brown but can't learn or considered not ready to learn in the White school system?

5. Why do the same poor children in SC have a different outcome in other areas like the Harlem Children's Zone or the Prep Academy Charter School in Connecticut that has closed the "achievement gap" between Black students and White students?

Letter # 5 – How Could America Get it so Wrong?

Dear Friend,

I feel like we have a relationship now. You are no longer just a "reader," we are friends trying to help our country recover from "race-ism" to make the changes that will be necessary to save our wonderful country for ourselves and our children!

How could America have totally missed the essence of *"A Nation at-Risk, 1983?"*

As a Black person I will give my opinion, this was the first time White people had ever been given a "diagnosis" like this one. The first reaction was shock, followed rather immediately with denial and then "projection!" (I think some would call it "scapegoating")

It became easy to say that report must be talking about poor Black people, the urban poor, anybody not doing well like regular White people; they became the "at-risk" group that all of the reform that followed was directed toward!

Well, we had a mis-diagnosis and everything that was "predicted" in the report has come true and we are still wondering what happened, why did it happen and what's going to happen now!

Most people have really forgotten about the report. And those who haven't still don't get it. For example, the report says that the children of this generation would not surpass the parents (for the first time in the history of America), they would not even reach or equal the achievements of the parents! I mention that to people like a doctor who after not being in touch for a long time, I inquired about his son who was such a fine young man when I first met him. Well, the father told me that his son after completing a year in college, had to put into a drug rehabilitation program. They are White and they live in a state that's predominantly White and score even below South Carolina. (Hint: the state starts with the letter "M" and ends with an "e")

I am so sad, I run into this all the time, and I feel so sad. I feel so sorry for White kids because their future is being ruined by the effects of "race-ism" in this country.

The "reform" that were tried to address the designated "at-risk" population didn't have an ounce of a chance to be successful and it wasn't.

Now that I really think about it, even if the true target of that report (White students) had been properly identified, the "normal bell curve standards" would have kept America from experiencing a positive response to that great warning that we got in 1983!

Let's go over that report again, with the knowledge that you now have from the previous Lessons, let's see if we can take a new approach!

Ms. Johnnie

SECTION 3
BEGINNING OF THE END

Lesson #5
A Nation-at-Risk, 1983
"Where Ignorance is Bliss, tis Folly to be Wise"

In 1983 we were given a WARNING that the American Education/ School System was raging war on our young, our country and our future. This is how the alarm was issued to us:

> *If an unfriendly foreign power had attempted to impose on America the mediocre educational performance that exists today, (1983) we might well have viewed it as an ACT OF WAR!*
>
> -A Nation –at-Risk: The Imperative for Educational Reform, April, 1983.

Well, I have to report to you today that America had already become a land of "bliss" so this extremely "wise" report was turned into a "folly" and the jokes began!

The education/school system was the "ENEMY." The American education/school system had done this to us, was continuing to do this and we let the American education/school system define the "enemy" and "how to fight back!"

This is really when the "folly" began!

The American education/school system said the report was talking about a certain "at-risk" population and that group must be the "poor Black students/people."

Are you laughing yet?

For the next 25 years the "enemy-education school system" gets lots of money to address the problem with the "at-risk population."

In 2009 we'll get to the "punch line." In 1983 the American students were ranked #5 (so alarming that it could be considered an attack by a foreign source) and now in 2009 we are approximately #31) America is on its knees and we still don't see the relationship between the error of interpretation in 1983 and today!

By now are you laughing so hard that you are "crying"!!!

Well, for those of you who are not in the state of "bliss" do you see why you are reading this book and what we have got to do to save our country?

At this point, I am going to review the report for those of us who are not drunk with "race-ism." Only an education/school system suffering from "superiority/inferiority intoxication" would direct twenty-five years of "reform" toward poor Black (inferior) students!

A Nation at-Risk was not talking about "poor Black children" or "poor Black people." Whenever a report of this magnitude is made, the report is addressing the "majority White population." Poor Black people were not even a twinkle in the eyes of this report. Blacks were not even mentioned as an aside.

A Nation at-risk was talking about the "country" and the entire "education/school system." At that point in time Whites made up approximately 80% of the population; and Blacks made up approximately 10%. This report was not talking about 50% of the 10% Blacks. (50% of Blacks are not poor so they were not in the at-risk group and therefore not targeted in the "reforms.")

The whole movement to reform the at-risk poor Black population doesn't even make sense even if the reform movement was successful with that group. If all of the 50% of the 13% Blacks became as smart and successful as Barack Obama or as rich as Oprah Winfrey, the severity of the warning would not have changed. The America education/school system would still put America at-risk!!!

This was a time when it would have made more sense to concentrate on the majority White student population which is who the report really was talking about. I am going to leave it to you to figure out why this decision was made to target the "poor Black students."

It truly was a nation-at-risk and twenty-five years later all of the predictions regarding what would happen to America if the warning was not heeded and corrections made, have now come true.

The twenty-five years of "reform" for the poor at-risk Black children have left America much worst off than where it was in 1983. (Lesson # 8- The 25th anniversary of *A Nation-at-Risk*)

What makes this mis-understanding so tragic is the fact that the reforms were completely wasted because the American education/school system did nothing of any value in their reform movement for the poor at-risk Black students.

Let's move on. Most of you have probably never heard of this report, and the rest of you have probably forgotten about it, consciously or unconsciously.

Here is summary of the report that was (and still is) an opportunity for us to "restart" the American education/school system to save ourselves, our country and our future.

Let's review the report together and pick up the discussion on the other side:

(Source: The Commission on Excellence in Education, 1983)

A Nation At-Risk, 1983

Our Nation is at risk. This report is concerned with only one of the many causes and dimensions of the problem, but it is the one that under girds American prosperity, security, and civility. The educational foundations of our society are presently being eroded by a rising tide of mediocrity that threatens our very future as a Nation and a people.

What was unimaginable a generation ago has begun to occur--others are matching and surpassing our educational attainments.

If an unfriendly foreign power had attempted to impose on America the mediocre educational performance that exists today, we might well have viewed it as an act of war. As it stands, we have allowed this to happen to ourselves. We have even squandered the gains in student achievement made in the wake of the Sputnik challenge. Moreover, we have dismantled essential support systems which helped make those gains possible. We have, in effect, been committing an act of unthinking, unilateral educational disarmament.

Our society and its educational institutions seem to have lost sight of the basic purposes of schooling, and of the high expectations and disciplined effort needed to attain them.

We seek to generate reform of our educational system in fundamental ways and to renew the Nation's commitment to schools and colleges of high quality throughout the length and breadth of our land.

That we have compromised this commitment is, upon reflection, hardly surprising, given the multitude of often conflicting demands we have placed on our Nation's schools and colleges. They are routinely called on to provide solutions to personal, social, and political problems that the home and other institutions either will not or cannot resolve. We must understand that these demands on our schools and colleges often exact an educational cost as well as a financial one.

We are confident that the American people, properly informed, will do what is right for their children and for the generations to come.

History is not kind to idlers. The time is long past when American's destiny was assured simply by an abundance of natural resources and inexhaustible human enthusiasm, and by our relative isolation from the malignant problems of older civilizations. The world is indeed one global village. We live among determined, well-educated, and strongly motivated competitors. We compete with them for international standing and markets, not only with products but also with the ideas of our laboratories and neighborhood workshops. America's position in the world may once have been reasonably secure with only a few exceptionally well-trained men and women. It is no longer.

Knowledge, learning, information, and skilled intelligence are the new raw materials of international commerce and are today spreading throughout the world as vigorously as miracle drugs, synthetic fertilizers, and blue jeans did earlier. If only to keep and improve on the slim competitive edge we still retain in world markets, we must dedicate ourselves to the reform of our educational system for the benefit of all-- old and young alike, affluent and poor, majority and minority. Learning is the indispensable investment required for success in the "information age" we are entering.

Our concern, however, goes well beyond matters such as industry and commerce. It also includes the intellectual, moral, and spiritual strengths of our people which knit together the very fabric of our society. The people of the United States need to know that individuals in our society who do not possess the levels of skill, literacy, and training essential to this new era will be effectively disenfranchised, not simply from the material rewards that accompany competent performance, but also from the chance to participate fully in our national life. A high level of shared education is essential to a free, democratic society and to the fostering of a common culture, especially in a country that prides itself on pluralism and individual freedom.

For our country to function, citizens must be able to reach some common understandings on complex issues, often on short notice and on the basis of conflicting or incomplete evidence. Education helps form these common understandings, a point Thomas Jefferson made long ago in his justly famous dictum:

I know no safe depository of the ultimate powers of the society but the people themselves; and if we think them not enlightened enough to exercise their control with a wholesome discretion, the remedy is not to take it from them but to inform their discretion.

Part of what is at risk is the promise first made on this continent: All, regardless of race or class or economic status, are entitled to a fair chance and to the tools for developing their individual powers of mind and spirit to the utmost. This promise means that all children by virtue of their own efforts, competently guided, can hope to attain the mature and informed judgment needed to secure gainful employment, and to manage their own lives, thereby serving not only their own interests but also the progress of society itself.

This is where we are for the first time:

- International comparisons of student achievement, completed a decade ago, reveal that on 19 academic tests American students were never first or second and, in comparison with other industrialized nations, were last seven times.

- Some 23 million American adults are functionally illiterate by the simplest tests of everyday reading, writing, and comprehension.

- About 13 percent of all 17-year-olds in the United States can be considered functionally illiterate. Functional illiteracy among minority youth may run as high as 40 percent.

- Average achievement of high school students on most standardized tests is now lower than 26 years ago when Sputnik was launched.

- Over half the populations of gifted students do not match their tested ability with comparable achievement in school.

- The College Board's Scholastic Aptitude Tests (SAT) demonstrate a virtually unbroken decline from 1963 to 1980. Average verbal scores fell over 50 points and average mathematics scores dropped nearly 40 points.

- College Board achievement tests also reveal consistent declines in recent years in such subjects as physics and English.

- Both the number and proportion of students demonstrating superior achievement on the SATs have also dramatically declined.

- Many 17-year-olds do not possess the "higher order" intellectual skills we should expect of them. Nearly 40 percent cannot draw inferences from written material; only one-fifth can write a persuasive essay; and only one-third can solve a mathematics problem requiring several steps.

- There was a steady decline in science achievement scores of U.S. 17-year-olds as measured by national assessments of science in 1969, 1973, and 1977.

- Between 1975 and 1980, remedial mathematics courses in public 4-year colleges increased by 72 percent and now constitute one-quarter of all mathematics courses taught in those institutions.

- Average tested achievement of students graduating from college is also lower.

- Business and military leaders complain that they are required to spend millions of dollars on costly remedial education and training programs in such basic skills as reading, writing, spelling, and computation. The Department of the Navy, for example, reported to the Commission that one-quarter of its recent recruits cannot read at the ninth grade level, the minimum needed simply to understand written safety instructions. Without remedial work they cannot even begin, much less complete, the sophisticated training essential in much of the modern military.

These deficiencies come at a time when the demand for highly skilled workers in new fields is accelerating rapidly. For example:

- Computers and computer-controlled equipment are penetrating every aspect of our lives--homes, factories, and offices.

- One estimate indicates that by the turn of the century millions of jobs will involve laser technology and robotics.

- Technology is radically transforming a host of other occupations. They include health care, medical science, energy production, food processing, construction, and the building, repair, and maintenance of sophisticated scientific, educational, military, and industrial equipment.

Analysts examining these indicators of student performance and the demands for new skills have made some chilling observations. Educational researcher Paul Hurd concluded at the end of a thorough national survey of student achievement that within the context of the modern scientific revolution, "We are raising a new generation of Americans that is scientifically and technologically illiterate." In a similar vein, John Slaughter, a former Director of the National Science Foundation, warned of "a growing chasm between a small scientific and technological elite and a citizenry ill-informed, indeed uninformed, on issues with a science component."

But the problem does not stop there, nor do all observers see it the same way. Some worry that schools may emphasize such rudiments as reading and computation at the expense of other essential skills such as comprehension, analysis, solving problems, and drawing conclusions. Still others are concerned that an over-emphasis on technical and occupational skills will leave little time for studying the arts and humanities that so enrich daily life, help maintain civility, and develop a sense of community. Knowledge of the humanities, they maintain, must be harnessed to science and technology if the latter are to remain creative and humane, just as the humanities need to be informed by science and technology if they are to remain relevant to the human condition. Another analyst, Paul Copperman, has drawn a sobering conclusion. Until now, he noted:

Each generation of Americans has outstripped its parents in education, in literacy, and in economic attainment. For the first time in the history of our country, the educational skills of one generation will not surpass, will not equal, will not even approach, those of their parents.

Statistics and their interpretation by experts show only the surface dimension of the difficulties we face. Beneath them lies a tension between hope and frustration that characterizes current attitudes about education at every level.

We have heard the voices of high school and college students, school board members, and teachers; of leaders of industry, minority groups, and higher education; of parents and State officials. We could hear the hope evident in their commitment to quality education and in their descriptions of outstanding programs and schools. We could also hear the intensity of their frustration, a growing impatience with shoddiness in many walks of American life, and the complaint that this shoddiness is too often reflected in our schools and colleges. Their frustration threatens to overwhelm their hope.

What lies behind this emerging national sense of frustration can be described as both a dimming of personal expectations and the fear of losing a shared vision for America.

On the personal level the student, the parent, and the caring teacher all perceive that a basic promise is not being kept. More and more young people emerge from high school ready neither for college nor for work. This predicament becomes more acute as the knowledge base continues its rapid expansion, the number of traditional jobs shrinks, and new jobs demand greater sophistication and preparation.

On the positive side is the significant movement by political and educational leaders to search for solutions--so far centering largely on the nearly desperate need for increased support for the teaching of mathematics and science. This movement is but a start on what we believe is a larger and more educationally encompassing need to improve teaching and learning in fields such as English, history, geography, economics, and foreign languages. **We believe this movement must be broadened and directed toward reform and excellence throughout education.**

Excellence in Education

We define "excellence" to mean several related things. At the level of the *individual learner*, it means performing on the boundary of individual ability in ways that test and push back personal limits, in school and in the workplace. Excellence characterizes a *school or college* that sets high expectations and goals for all learners, then tries in every way possible to help students reach them. Excellence characterizes a *society* that has adopted these policies, for it will then be prepared through the education and skill of its people to respond to the challenges of a rapidly changing world. Our Nation's people and its schools and colleges must be committed to achieving excellence in all these senses.

We do not believe that a public commitment to excellence and educational reform must be made at the expense of a strong public commitment to the equitable treatment of our diverse population. The twin goals of equity and high-quality schooling have profound and practical meaning for our economy and society, and we cannot permit one to yield to the other either in principle or in practice. To do so would deny young people their chance to learn and live according to their aspirations and abilities. It also would lead to a generalized accommodation to mediocrity in our society on the one hand or the creation of an undemocratic elitism on the other.

Our goal must be to develop the talents of all to their fullest. Attaining that goal requires that we expect and assist all students to work to the limits of their capabilities. We should expect schools to have genuinely high standards rather than minimum ones, and parents to support and encourage their children to make the most of their talents and abilities.

The search for solutions to our educational problems must also include a commitment to life-long learning. The task of rebuilding our system of learning is enormous and must be properly understood and taken seriously: Although a million and a half new workers enter the economy each year from our schools and colleges, the adults working today will still make up about 75 percent of the workforce in the year 2000.

These workers, and new entrants into the workforce, will need further education and retraining if they--and we as a Nation--are to thrive and prosper.

The Learning Society

In a world of ever-accelerating competition and change in the conditions of the workplace, of ever-greater danger, and of ever-larger opportunities for those prepared to meet them, educational reform should focus on the goal of creating a Learning Society. At the heart of such a society is the commitment to a set of values and to a system of education that affords all members the opportunity to stretch their minds to full capacity, from early childhood through adulthood, learning more as the world itself changes. Such a society has as a basic foundation the idea that education is important not only because of what it contributes to one's career goals but also because of the value it adds to the general quality of one's life. Also at the heart of the Learning Society are educational opportunities extending far beyond the traditional institutions of learning, our schools and colleges. They extend into homes and workplaces; into libraries, art galleries, museums, and science centers; indeed, into every place where the individual can develop and mature in work and life. In our view, formal schooling in youth is the essential foundation for learning throughout one's life. But without life-long learning, one's skills will become rapidly dated.

In contrast to the ideal of the Learning Society, however, we find that for too many people education means doing the minimum work necessary for the moment, then coasting through life on what may have been learned in its first quarter. But this should not surprise us because we tend to express our educational standards and expectations largely in terms of "minimum requirements." And where there should be a coherent continuum of learning, we have none, but instead an often incoherent, outdated patchwork quilts. Many individual, sometimes heroic, examples of schools and colleges of great merit do exist. Our findings and testimony confirm the vitality of a number of notable schools and programs, but their very distinction stands out against a vast mass shaped by tensions and pressures that inhibit systematic academic and vocational achievement for the majority of students. In some metropolitan areas basic literacy has become the goal rather than the starting point. In some colleges maintaining enrollments is of greater day-to-day concern than maintaining rigorous academic standards. And the ideal of academic excellence as the primary goal of schooling seems to be fading across the board in American education.

Thus, we issue this call to all who care about America and its future: to parents and students; to teachers, administrators, and school board members; to colleges and industry; to union members and military leaders; to governors and State legislators; to the President; to members of Congress and other public officials; to members of learned and scientific societies; to the print and electronic media; to concerned citizens everywhere. America is at risk.

We are confident that America can address this risk. If the tasks we set forth are initiated now and our recommendations are fully realized over the next several years, we can expect reform of our Nation's schools, colleges, and universities. This would also reverse the current declining trend--a trend that stems more from weakness of purpose, confusion of vision, underuse of talent, and lack of leadership, than from conditions beyond our control.

The Tools at Hand

It is our conviction that the essential raw materials needed to reform our educational system are waiting to be mobilized through effective leadership:

- the natural abilities of the young that cry out to be developed and the undiminished concern of parents for the well-being of their children;

- the commitment of the Nation to high retention rates in schools and colleges and to full access to education for all;

- the persistent and authentic American dream that superior performance can raise one's state in life and shape one's own future;

- the dedication, against all odds, that keeps teachers serving in schools and colleges, even as the rewards diminish;

- our better understanding of learning and teaching and the implications of this knowledge for school practice, and the numerous examples of local success as a result of superior effort and effective dissemination;

- the ingenuity of our policymakers, scientists, State and local educators, and scholars in formulating solutions once problems are better understood;

- the traditional belief that paying for education is an investment in ever-renewable human resources that are more durable and flexible than capital plant and equipment, and the availability in this country of sufficient financial means to invest in education;

- the equally sound tradition, from the Northwest Ordinance of 1787 until today, that the Federal Government should supplement State, local, and other resources to foster key national educational goals; and

- the voluntary efforts of individuals, businesses, and parent and civic groups to cooperate in strengthening educational programs.

These raw materials, combined with the unparalleled array of educational organizations in America, offer us the possibility to create a Learning Society, in which public, private, and parochial schools; colleges and universities; vocational and technical schools and institutes; libraries; science centers, museums, and other cultural institutions; and corporate training and retraining programs offer opportunities and choices for all to learn throughout life.

The Public's Commitment

... This country was built on American respect for education. . . Our challenge now is to create a resurgence of that thirst for education that typifies our Nation's history.

The most recent (1982) Gallup Poll of the *Public's Attitudes Toward the Public Schools* strongly supported a theme heard during our hearings: People are steadfast in their belief that education is the major foundation for the future strength of this country. They even considered education more important than developing the best industrial system or the strongest military force, perhaps because they understood education as the cornerstone of both. They also held that education is "extremely important" to one's future success, and that public education should be the top priority for additional Federal funds. Education occupied first place among 12 funding categories considered in the survey--above health care, welfare, and military defense, with 55 percent selecting public education as one of their first three choices. Very clearly, the public understands the primary importance of education as the foundation for a satisfying life, an enlightened and civil society, a strong economy, and a secure Nation.

At the same time, the public has no patience with undemanding and superfluous high school offerings. In another survey, more than 75 percent of all those questioned believed every student planning to go to college should take 4 years of mathematics, English, history/U.S. government, and science, with more than 50 percent adding 2 years each of a foreign language and economics or business. The public even supports requiring much of this curriculum for students who do not plan to go to college. These standards far exceed the strictest high school graduation requirements of any State today, and they also exceed the admission standards of all but a handful of our most selective colleges and universities.

Another dimension of the public's support offers the prospect of constructive reform. The best term to characterize it may simply be the honorable word "patriotism." Citizens know intuitively what some of the best economists have shown in their research that education is one of the chief engines of a society's material well-being. They know, too, that education is the common bond of a pluralistic society and helps tie us to other cultures around the globe. Citizens also know in their bones that the safety of the United States depends principally on the wit, skill, and spirit of a self-confident people, today and tomorrow. It is, therefore, essential--especially in a period of long-term decline in educational achievement--for government at all levels to affirm its responsibility for nurturing the Nation's intellectual capital.

And perhaps most important, citizens know and believe that the meaning of America to the rest of the world must be something better than it seems to many today. Americans like to think of this Nation as the preeminent country for generating the great ideas and material benefits for all mankind. The citizen is dismayed at a steady 15-year decline in industrial productivity, as one great American industry after another falls to world competition. The citizen wants the country to act on the belief, expressed in our hearings and by the large majority in the Gallup Poll that education should be at the top of the Nation's agenda. ###

What do you think? Was America asleep? Was America drunk or had ignorance already consumed everyone?

That report is the best report I have ever read in America. I think it goes one step ahead of the "Declaration of Independence!" It clearly outlined the problem, how to address it and clearly defined the goal and the consequences.

In my native Gullah language I would say, *A Nation-at-Risk* be fa true…

At this point I would recommend that you research all of the "reforms" that followed the 1983 report for the next 25 years. Be sure to pay particular attention to who is classified as "at-risk" and what reforms proceeded…

I will share with you some "responses" that have come to my attention that I would like to share with you as we move toward the twenty-fifth anniversary of the 1983, A –Nation-at-Risk. (Lesson #8)

Jeff Howard of The Efficacy Institute, Inc. in April of 1991 says:

Our approach to educating children is failing because the attitudes that underlie it are wrong. American beliefs about human intelligence and educability are limiting and counterproductive; they represent a major constraint on the development of our young, and an entirely inappropriate basis for 21st century pedagogy. As the "American Century" draws to a close to the tune of the emerging economic hegemony of Japan, we confront a highly competitive global economic order that demands ever-increasing levels of literacy and problem solving proficiency in workers. In response, we are raising children whose knowledge and skills are inferior to those of their industrial-age parents. The recent heightened attention of politicians and business leaders provides a clue about the seriousness and breadth of the national concern over this issue. The fact that no workable approach to national educational reform has yet surfaced indicates the depth of our muddle. After years of flailing about, looking for scapegoats and making empty demands for change, it is clear that something is interfering with our capacity to mobilize our resources and our know-how to educate children. The obstruction lies at the most fundamental level of our thinking about people and their capabilities: we operate from the self-fulfilling conviction that only a small percentage of children are intelligent enough to become well educated. This belief has a profoundly negative impact on our pedagogy, engenders lack of confidence in children and indifference to data that demonstrates that virtually all of them can learn, and it discourages mobilization of an effective movement for educational reform.

It is not as if we lack models of success – examples abound of school interventions that work. Jaime Escalante has taught calculus to some of the poorest children in Los Angeles. In his thirteen year tenure as Community Superintendent in Brooklyn, Jerome Harris presided over significant improvements in the academic performance of some of the poorest schools in New York...

I also strongly feel that nobody wants to put the "responsibility" for educating our children on the school system. Here we are over twenty-five

*years later no one wants to put the responsibility at the feet of the school
system. It's the American education/school system that must be "restarted."
Defending or protecting the teachers is not helping anybody. The teachers
are victim of this toxic system as well.*

*Why do you think we are resisting the notion that the American school
system is the "problem" that needs to be fixed?*

*Our well being and our future are not going to be "kind to idlers,"
"liars," and Americans under the influence of "superiority/inferiority
intoxication."*

*This nation does not become a nation at risk because of poorly educated
Black students!*

*I care and for that reason I have set out to tell you why Johnny and Josie
can't read, write, compute or think critically. It's the American education/
school system that has to be stopped in its tracks and be "restarted."*

Education is too important for us to let this system continue to go on.

*My passion, as you know, comes from my history, it is education that has
brought my people, my family, out of chattel slavery and into the marvelous
light of freedom. Education is too important to America and to our world.
I will not give up on America's future. That passion for education still lives
in me as great as the day my forefathers clung unto that passion as their sole
possession as they crossed the line from being so poor they did not even own
themselves, to where we are today. All of our young people today, majority
(superior) culture and minority (inferior) culture we must embrace this new
millennium as my people did following the passage of the 13th Amendment
in 1865. As my people became free to pursue their future, our young people
must pursue their future in this new millennium that gave us ownership
of ourselves. That passion of 1865 still lives within me. I must pass it on. I
will pass it on to those of you who care.*

*The findings in these Lessons are based mainly on what I have learned,
experienced and observed in my lifetime as a poor Black woman. Only
because I come from that background, I am fortunate to have the perspective
and knowledge that I can now share with you.*

*As a Black student in the South of the fifties and sixties, I received my
education in the Black school system from pre-school through college. From
the seventies on I have received graduate and post-graduate school from the
White school system. I have been a teacher in the Black school system and the
White school system. I was a child and received parenting while a student*

in the Black school system and participated as a parent in the White school system where my two children attended.

I see the whole cow. I am fortunate to have been in the right place at the right time. It is with great humility that I offer to you why the public system of this country puts this Nation at risk. I continue to welcome you to this personal and intellectual adventure where we are exploring the facts and will explore truth together.

If you always do...what you've always done...you'll always get...what you already have!

And we keep doing what we do so we have kept what we had...

Shortly after the tenth anniversary of *A Nation-at-Risk, 1983*, Dr. Thomas Sowell, an economist and senior fellow at the Hoover Institution in Stanford, California calls the education system in the June 6, 1994 issue of *Forbes*, a "Tragicomedy":

At this point let's go back to A Nation-at-Risk, 1983. In 1983 when this came out I can remember the news media doing a fantastic job of getting the report out to the people. What happened? Why did America totally drop the ball and just went on with life. This is not what the report thought would happen. The report speaks of great confidence in the American people and how the report would be used to address and correct the problems. That did not happen. The public accepted the school system's response (poor at-risk Black students) and the rest they say is history.

Twenty-five years later the media didn't even bother reporting the findings of the 25th anniversary. So when the 25th anniversary of the report came out last year as far as I know it got no media coverage and most people would not have known what it was about anyway.

Luckily, I again was at the right place at the right time and was able to get a copy of the 25th anniversary report.

History is not kind to idlers, liars, and people suffering from "superior/inferior intoxication." Why do you think this report was ignored?

Again, A Nation –at-Risk was referring to the majority in the American school system. The report was in other words talking about the education of White children.

People have ignored the report, picked out poor Black and urban children, labeled them as the "at-risk population" and continued to rearrange the chairs on the Titanic!

What did we miss in 1983? How did we miss it? Why did we miss it?

As I have noted, this report really has the answer we seek to address the condition of where we are twenty-five years later.

For that reason I am going to go over this report one more time. We have got to fully appreciate the "wisdom" of this document:

Who presented the report?

It was presented by the National Commission on Excellence in Education created and directed to present a report on the quality of education in America...

What was the purpose of the report?

The purpose: to help define the problems afflicting American education and to provide solutions, not search for scapegoats.

The Commission believed that problems could be both understood and corrected if the people, together with those who have public responsibility, care enough and are courageous enough to do what is required.

What was the makeup of the Commission that devised the report?

The Commission represented a diverse group of persons to examine one of the central issues which will define our Nation's future.

Was the report political?

A report free of political partisanship.

What was the goal and objectives of the report?

Assesses the quality of teaching and learning in our Nation's public and private schools, colleges, and universities.

Compared American schools and colleges with those of other advanced nations.

Studied the relationship between college admissions requirements and student achievement in high school.

Identified educational programs which result in notable student success in college.

Assessed the degree to which major social and educational changes in the last quarter of the last century have affected achievement.

Defined problems which must be faced and overcome if we are successfully to pursue the course of excellence in education.

The Commission's charter directed it to pay particular attention to teenage youth, focused largely on high schools.

Selective attention was given to the formative years spent in elementary schools, to higher education, and to vocational and technical programs.

With the diversity and difference of opinion the report gave evidence that men and women of good will can agree on common goals and on ways to pursue them.

What was the guiding belief behind the report?

They believed that:

All regardless of race or class or economic status, are entitled to a fair chance and the tools of developing their individual powers of mind and spirit to the utmost. This promise means that all children by virtue of their own efforts, competently guided, can hope to attain the mature and informed judgment needed to secure gainful employment, and to manage their own interests and also the progress of society itself.

What was the conclusion of findings in the report?

Our Nation is at Risk...

What role did "Education" play in putting our country at Risk?

The report concerned itself with only one of the many causes and dimensions of the problem, which they stated, "undergirds American prosperity, security and civility. Education. That while we can take justifiable pride in what our schools and colleges have historically accomplished and contributed to the United States and the well-being of our people, the educational foundations of our society are presently being eroded by a rising tide of mediocrity that threatens our very future as a nation and a people.

What signals are our students exhibiting regarding the risk that the nation faces?

What was unimaginable a generation ago has begun to occur – others are matching and surpassing our educational attainments:

- If an unfriendly foreign power had attempted to impose on America the mediocre educational performance that exists today, we might well have viewed it as an act of war!
- As it stands, we have allowed this to happen to ourselves.
- We have even squandered the gains in student achievement made in the wake of the Sputnik challenge.
- We have dismantled essential support systems which helped make those gains possible.
- We have, in effect, been committing an act of unthinking, unilateral educational disarmament.

- Our society and its educational institutions seem to have lost sight of the basic purposes of schooling, and of the high expectations and disciplined efforts needed to attain them.

- Reform our educational system in fundamental ways and to renew the Nation's commitment to schools and colleges of high quality throughout.

- THAT WE HAVE COMPROMISED THIS COMMITMENT IS, UPON REFLECTION, HARDLY SURPRISING, GIVEN THE MULTITUDE OF OFTEN CONFLICTING DEMANDS WE HAVE PLACED ON OUR Nation's schools and colleges

- They are routinely trying to provide solutions to personal, social, and political problems that the home and other institutions either will not or cannot resolve.

- These demands on our schools and colleges exact an educational cost as well as a financial one.

What is "THE RISK?"

- History is not kind to idlers

- Time is long past when America's destiny was assured simply be an abundance of natural resources and inexhaustible human enthusiasm, and by our relative isolation from the malignant problems of older civilizations

- The world is indeed, one global village

- We live among determined, well-educated, and strongly motivated competitors

- Knowledge, learning, information, and skilled intelligence are the new raw materials of international commerce and are today spreading throughout the world

- If only to keep and improve on the slim competitive edge we still retain in world markets, we must dedicate ourselves to the reform of our educational system for the benefit of all —old and young, affluent and poor, majority and minority

• Learning is the indispensable investment required for success in the "information age" we were entering

What are the INDICATORS OF THE RISK?

1. International comparisons of student achievement

2. The number of functional illiterates, tested by the simplest tests of everyday reading, writing, and comprehension, in the adult population and the group of 17 year-olds

3. Average achievement of high school students on most standardized tests compared to 36 years ago when Sputnik was launched

4. Over half the population of gifted students do not match their tested ability with comparable achievement in school

5. Decline in SAT scores from 1963, and other declines

6. Number and proportion of students demonstrating superior achievement on the SATs have also declined

7. Many seniors do not possess the "higher order" intellectual skills we should expect of them. Cannot draw inferences from written material; write a persuasive essay and solve a mathematical problem requiring several steps

8. Decline in science achievement scores

9. Increase in remedial mathematics courses

10. Average tested achievement of students graduating from college is also lower

11. Business and military leaders complain about the costly remedial education and training programs for such basic skills such as reading, writing, spelling and computation

12. These deficiencies come at a time when the demand for highly skilled workers in new fields is accelerating rapidly.

What are some of the alarming examples of our predicament?

- "We are raising a new generation of Americans that is scientifically, and technologically illiterate."

- A growing chasm between a small scientific and technological elite and a citizenry ill-informed, indeed uninformed, on issues with a scientific component

- Each generation of Americans has outstripped its parents in education, in literacy, and in economic attainment. For the first time in the history of our country, the educational skills of one generation will not surpass, will not equal, will not even approach, those of their parents.

- The average graduate of our schools and colleges today is not as well-educated as the average graduate of 35 or 45 years ago, when a much smaller proportion of our population completed high school and college

What is the mood of the people regarding the state of the country?

We also hear the intensity of their frustration, a growing impatience with shoddiness in many walks of American life, and the complaint that shoddiness is too often reflected in our schools and colleges. Their frustration threatens to overwhelm their hope.

What lies behind this emerging national sense of frustration can be described as both a dimming of personal expectations and the fear of losing a shared vision for America

On the personal level the student, the parent, and the caring teacher all perceive that a basic promise is not being kept

What is the condition of our graduates?

More and more young people emerge from high school ready neither for college nor for work. This predicament becomes more acute as the knowledge base continues its rapid expansion; the predicament must be properly understood and taken seriously

How did the report classify EXCELLENCE IN EDUCATION?

- We define "excellence" to mean several related things. At the level of the individual learner, it means performing on the boundary of individual ability in ways that test and push back personal limits, in school and the workplace

- Excellence characterizes a school or college that sets high expectations and goals for all learners, then tries in every way possible to help students reach them

- Excellence characterizes a society that has adopted these policies, for it will then be prepared through the education and skill of its people to respond to the challenges of a rapidly changing world

- Our nation's people and its schools and colleges must be committed to achieving excellence in all these senses

- Our goal must be to develop the talents of all to their fullest. Attaining that goal requires that we expect and assist all students to work to the limits of their capabilities

- We should expect schools to have genuinely high standards rather than minimum ones, and parents to support and encourage their children to make the most of their talents and abilities

- The search for solutions to our educational problems must include a commitment to life-long learning

- The task of rebuilding our system of learning is enormous and be properly understood and taken seriously

Why was THE LEARNING SOCIETY there vision for America?

Such a society has a basic foundation the idea that education is important not only because of what it contributes to one's career goals but also because of the value it adds to the general quality of one's life

For too many people education means doing the minimum work necessary for the moment, and then coasting through life on what may have been learned in its first quarter

The ideal of academic excellence as the primary goal of school seems to be fading across the board in American education

Thus, we issue this call to all who care about America and its future: to parents and students; to teachers, administrators, and school board members; to colleges and industry; state legislators; to the President; to members of Congress and other public officials; to members of learned and scientific societies; to the print and electronic media; to concerned citizens everywhere. America is at risk.

What did they think caused our at-risk predicament?

1. Weakness of purpose
2. Confusion of vision
3. Underuse of talent
4. Lack of leadership
5. All are conditions within our control

What were THE TOOLS AT HAND to address our predicament?

Effective Leadership can mobilize the essential raw materials that are available and waiting to reform our educational system

What are the assets as we address our deficits?

1. the natural abilities of the young that cry out to be developed and the undiminished concern of parents for the well-being of their children;
2. the commitment of the Nation to high retention rates in schools and colleges and to full access to education for all;

3. the persistent and authentic American dream that superior performance can raise one's state in life and shape one's own future;

4. the dedication, against all odds, that keep teachers serving in schools and colleges, even as the rewards diminish;

5. our better understanding of learning and teaching and the implications of this knowledge for school practice, and the numerous examples of local success as a result of superior effort and effective dissemination;

6. the ingenuity of our policymakers, scientists, State and local educators, and scholars in formulating solutions once problems are better understood;

7. the traditional belief that paying for education is an investment in ever-renewable human resources that are more durable and flexible than capital plant and equipment, and the availability in this country of sufficient financial means to invest in education;

8. the equally sound tradition, from the Northwest Ordinance of 1787 until today, that the Federal Government should supplement State, local and other resources to foster key national educational goals; and

9. the voluntary efforts of individuals, businesses, and parent and civic groups to cooperate in strengthening educational programs.

Recommendations are based on what principles?

1. "Our recommendations are based on the beliefs that everyone can learn"

2. "That everyone is born with an 'urge' to learn which can be nurtured"

3. "That a solid high school education is within the reach of virtually all"

4. "And that life-long learning will equip people with skills required for new careers and for citizenship"

As we leave this lesson, the conclusion looks something like this:

American schools are in a mess. If you don't already know this, just take a look at the bleak statistics that have emerged over the past ten years. Kids simply aren't learning. They are pulling down more A's and B's than ever before because of inflated grades, but they're not getting an education. They can't organize a paragraph (much less an essay); identify Winston Churchill (much less Charlemagne); read Dickens (much less Shakespeare); understand main ideas in a text (much less infer meanings); separate major issues in a political campaign (much less handle their ambiguity); name the capital of Germany (much less find Iraq on a map); or calculate percentages (much less figure out the cost per item in the supermarket). Besides, SATs and comprehension scores are falling; truancy and dropout rates are rising; and our unanswered cries for help are getting louder.

-from Save our Schools by Mary Susan Miller

I will paraphrase with one thing, I would change that last statement to, "and the unanswered cries for help are getting more silent" as we go along in the twenty-first century...

Just recently we learned that the majority of America's students do not know who George Washington is. Someone wrote into CNN or MSNBC that he didn't know why that was such a big deal.

This is my response to that young man: Even if you don't think it's important for students to know the first President of this country, let's look at the real significance of this new revelation: In every school in this country, every student from K-12 is trying to get their students to know about "George Washington" and the American school system has not been successful! If the American education/school system cannot teach students about George Washington, what should we do now?

In conclusion, this is what I believe:

When A Nation at Risk, 1983 came out, America could not believe that report was talking about "successful" Americans (White Americans) they felt the report must have been talking about poor, Blacks, the underclass. So for twenty-five years we have spent all of our time concentrating all of our efforts and resources on the "at-risk" population.

That report was describing the state of Whites in America!

Since America processed that report incorrectly, America has suffered the consequences. For twenty-five years the reform was directed incorrectly and now we are worse off than ever!

Lesson #5 – Facts that Need to be Independently Investigated

1. How did the country respond to the 1983 Report, *A Nation at Risk*?

2. What population did the "at-risk" designation apply?

3. Was this report referring to "minorities?"

4. What has changed since the report for American education?

5. How do most Americans rate American education?

6. How do most Americans feel their children are doing?

7. Do they think the education their children are getting will prepare them for a successful life?

8. Do Americans think there is any relationship between this report, A Nation at Risk and the state of America's economic problems

9. Does the "normal bell curve" mask the true state of American education?

10. What needs to happen to change the findings in the report?

Letter #6 – There's Black Talk and there's White Talk

Dear Readers,

When the American education/school system labeled the "poor Black students" as the target group in response to *A Nation at-risk*, the message never even got to that group because the school system didn't recognize the language of that group and that group certainly didn't speak "White" so they didn't even try to understand what the school system was saying. They stayed in school as long as they could and then they dropped out, took the pipeline to prison and went on with their life!

So the 25 years of "reform" gives us the products of the Chicago school system where students now treat people the way the school system has treated and continues to treat them. Children will learn no matter what. They learn best by the way they are treated and see how their group is treated. This is played out in every "hood" in every city in this country. Twenty-five years of "reform" on a group that they couldn't even communicate with.

Things got so mixed up that Jesse Jackson and Ed Koch ended up on the same side against "Black English Only" students. Language is now the new mode of "discrimination."

When I invited you to join me on this journey, I assured you that my life experiences have equipped me for this journey and I would share everything I have learned so we can be prepared to lead the "restart" the American education/school system to save ourselves, our children and our country.

When Blacks were brought here they were never "taught" English. In most cases Africans from different villages and different countries had to "create" their own language when they got to America. They created a major language that's today called "Gullah/Geechee". Other names today are Black English, African American Vernacular English, Hip Hop, and other variations. Most Black people are aware of this fact and speak it or understand it.

When we got our freedom after the Civil War, we embraced education and "learned" mainstream American English if we were going to be successful. The Black Education System did a very good job. Blacks made great strides in every walk of life!

Then the passage of Brown vs. the Board of Education changed the role of education for poor Blacks. On the surface it looked like a victory but for a group of Blacks who got left in the urban and rural areas of this country that still needed to learn the value of an education and the language of success, they were locked in a vicious cycle of poverty speaking only the Black language and thinking that the other language is "White Talk" and they have no interest in speaking the language of the "enemy."

So we end up with a segment of the population that is a liability at a time when we need them to be the asset that they could become if we can get "race-ism" out of the discourse.

As a Black person many Whites may not be able to understand the way I express things.

In the meantime, those of you who can understand me, let's soldier on to understand how "race-ism" keeps some Blacks from getting an education more effectively now than when it was against the law to educate a Black slave!

Ms. Johnnie

Lesson #6

Speaking of Inferiority
"Dis Nation be at-risk real bad now and Ed Koch and Jesse Jackson sa' nuten ain't be wrong with dat!"

You Lie!

Any Black person who speaks like that in South Carolina is not going to be elected to any office in the state. He would be accused of speaking "ebonics"...

A White person can be elected to the U.S. House of Representative! (He's speaking "southern")

Language is Power!

The power can be given or denied to children who don't speak mainstream American English (White) and that is what this lesson is going to cover.

I think the election of Barack Obama is more proof of that than anything. His command of words won him the election to the highest office in the World!

Command of the language has made Oprah Winfrey one of the wealthiest women in the World!

Color and "race" has finally been trumped by "language."

Dr. Martin Luther King, Jr. in his "I Have a Dream Speech" wished that his four "Black" children would not be judged by the color of their skins but by the countenance of their character.

More than anything today, the "power" today is in the hands of those who have command of the "language!"

During the period after the Civil War, ex-slaves used education to rise. With all of the obstacles, hurdles and hardships they endured knowing that education was the way to the Promised Land...

In the Blacks schools, the Blacks teachers, with little education they knew that the difference between an educated and an uneducated person was in the "words." If one closed his or her eyes, you could hear Black or

White and educated Black or uneducated Black. One did not need an IQ test to predict who was going to be successful and who was not.

When Blacks left the South during the great migration, after only a couple of weeks, they adopted a different way of speaking, not to be identified with the "ignorant" one from the South. So if a relative returned for a visit to the South in little more than a couple of weeks, he was speaking "proper" and I mean p-r-o-p-e-e-r-r!

"If the misery of our poor be caused not by the laws of nature, but by our institutions, great is our sin."

-Charles Darwin

Language prejudice remains a "legitimate" prejudice.

"How's Education?" O! E Bin Dead..."

Education
Be
Resting
In
PEACE
Skool

"A lie gets halfway around the world before the truth has a chance to put its pants on."

Winston Churchill
(1874-1965)

Let's give truth a try...

Today when a Black child opens his mouth and speaks anything other than "mainstream American English" you know his past, his present and his future. He is not doing well on his standardized tests at school; his parents and grandparents probably speak like he does and they didn't do well in school and are probably not doing well in life right now.

Education for that population is DOA (dead-on-arrival)!

How did they get left behind when other Blacks figuratively speaking "migrated" to "mainstream American English" and climbed the ladder to reach the American dream?

This is my theory regarding what happened.

During the period between the Civil War and the Civil Rights Movement (particularly the passage of Brown vs. the Board of Education) Blacks lived in segregated communities where there was a combination of "schooled," speakers of "mainstream American English" and "Black Language;" and un-schooled, speakers of "Black Language ONLY."

There were the professional Blacks and Black business owners whose families knew the value of "education" and had used education to do well in the American society in spite of the "Jim Crow Laws" that enforced separation. There was a group that still had not embraced "education" and spoke the Black Language-Only.

I am going to simplify that period in history because we have a lot to cover in this Lesson but the main thing to know about that period is there was always a "class" difference in the Black communities based on language.

Then after Brown vs. the Board of Education/the Civil Rights Movement with the changes in housing laws, the "successful" Black who were prepared and ready to enter mainstream America, they moved out of the inner cities and bought houses in the "White suburbs."

The Urban/Ghetto Community Emerges Throughout America

This left the group that spoke our Black Language-ONLY, who had not embraced education as an opportunity/responsibility to pursue the American Dream locked into the inner city with no clue regarding a way out or where or how the others had mysteriously left. To make things even worse, the Black school system that catered to helping Blacks learn the value of education, how to pursue education and how to use it to "make it" in the "White man's world" was locked up, shut down and teachers fired. The newly in-charge "White school system" was now in charge of poor (needing free and reduced lunch and breakfast) Black children, who spoke a "foreign language" didn't show any interest in school and the parents were no-show at PTA or any parent-teacher conferences. When they showed up they spoke the same *"funny language"* and only seemed to show up when they thought their child had been unfairly treated, ready to fight.

These pockets of "Black Language-Only" speakers were found all over this country

While the "Black Language" originated in the South, at the end of the Civil War and particularly after the rise of the KKK and "Jim Crow Laws," Blacks migrated to large cities throughout this country. They took their language with them and they congregated together in their own "segregated" areas. These later became designated as "urban" and/or "ghetto."

How Were Schools Educating this Population?

Well, I, like you, didn't have this reach my radar until "The Media" told us that the school board of education wanted to use federal money to "teach ebonics" to the Black students in the urban area of Oakland, California.

When I looked into the entire Oakland issue, I came to a completely different understanding of what was actually happening.

The Story of Oakland and the "Ebonics" Case According to Me

In Oakland, as in most urban areas populated by poor Blacks speaking Black Language Only (BLO) the students in that area was not doing well. Other minorities, Asian and Hispanic were doing better than the BLO Blacks.

A very smart Chairman of the Board in that school district was a Black woman who looked at the situation and observed that non-native Mainstream American English speakers (Spanish, Japanese, etc.) students were first enrolled in English as a Second Language (ESOL) classes. After becoming proficient in MAE they were then given "placement" tests and they went on and did well in school.

The situation was completely different for the Black students. Blacks, as soon as they reached the schools they were given the "placement test" in MAE and they predominantly ended in special education classes.

She acknowledged a fact that the Black students were not native MAE speakers either so what if these students were first put in ESOL classes like the other non-native MAE speakers and then given the placement tests in MAE they would have a chance to go to regular classes and do well like the other ESOL recipients.

The Media Got it Wrong, Jesse Jackson Got it Wrong and the Rest is History

This was a turning point in the history of education for BLO Black students. This group of Blacks was "locked" out of the opportunity to get an education and locked into the cycle of poverty and now we see the results of locking people into an area because they do not speak the "language of school" and the schools have been "sanctioned" by the following important people to deny this group the opportunity "to learn the language of school" and therefore try to get an education:

Jesse Jackson
Rush Limbaugh
Maya Angelou
Kweisi Mfume
Mario Cuomo
Ed Koch
Henry Louis Gates, Jr.
Eldridge Cleaver
Bill Cosby
Ralph Abernathy III
Shelby Steele
William Bennett
Richard Riley

The Most Bizarre Thing I've Ever Seen in My Life

This was the most bizarre thing I have ever seen in my life. Blacks, Whites, Liberal, Conservative and in-betweens took the mis-interpretation provided by **THE MEDIA** *and eagerly stopped a promising opportunity to give BLO Black students an opportunity to get an education.*

How is it that long-time civil rights organizations and activists ended up on the same side of the barricade with their traditional adversaries?

Approximately ten years later the only thing we've heard from that group is Bill Cosby's indignation that some young Black people are going around speaking "an unknown language" to him and not doing well in school. That furthermore when he spoke to the boy's father, the father spoke that same "unknown language" and was showing no interest in buying "hooked on phonics" for his son.

Bill Cosby calls it time to air our dirty laundry for the good of everybody.

Dirty Laundry Time! For Dr. Cosby

Since Mr. Cosby believes in publicly airing our dirty laundry. I will take this opportunity to tell him what I think of his ideas and approach! He is wrong, his ideas are a sick joke and he should stick to comedy!

Don't come out as a scholar, an educator, spewing venom based on ignorance!

Thank goodness for one thing, the parents and children he is making a hit off right now are totally unaware of what he is saying about them!

The people who are raving over Mr. Cosby's words are the ones who left the "Black community" after the Civil Rights Movement and never returned to see what happened to those who were left behind.

BLO Black Students Have to be Taught English as a Second Language

Well, since the group listed above was so successful in stopping BLO-Black children from getting the opportunity to learn MAE as a second language, they are still disproportionately in special education or not learning very well because the educational system is in MAE and the students are BLO so you either have the teachers correcting the students which shuts a student down very quickly or some systems choose to ignore the fact that there students are speaking a "different" language.

This is an example of what's happening in some Title I/No Child Left Behind Schools in the South-The teacher is trying to "communicate"

in one Language and the child is trying to "communicate" in another language and there is "no communication" between the two:

Black Language-Only/School Language

Teacher enters with an African American child. It appears the teacher wants to telephone the child's parents.

The teacher looks up at the student and says:

Teacher: "Bobby, what does your mother do everyday?"

Bobby: "She *be* at home!"

Teacher: "You mean, she *is* at home," (the teacher corrects Bobby)

Bobby: "No, she ain't, cause she took my grandmother to the hospital this morning."

Teacher: "You know what I meant. You are not supposed to say, 'she *be* at home.' You are to say, 'she *is* at home."

Bobby: "Why you trying to make me lie? She ain't at home."

Teacher: "You are being very disrespectful, don't you want to learn, you say what I tell you to say right now or I'm taking you to the principal's office!

Bobby: (mumbles something under his breath, gives the teacher a "are you crazy look" – you ain't goin to make me lie!)

They go to the Principal's office.

Teacher:	"Bobby is being disrespectful again. I want him suspended. I try to teach him and he fights me everyday."
Principal:	"I'm going to call your mother." He dials and waits. "There is no answer at your home number."
Bobby:	"I tell you Mr. Principal, this teacher, she be crazy, she be trippin'. I tell her my mother ain't at home, she be at the hospital with my grandma."
Teacher:	"Why did you tell me 'she is at home'?"
Bobby:	"I ain't tell you dat, I say she be at home everyday, when you ax me way she be in the daytime. Then you ax me way she be today and I tell you she be at the hospital wit my grandma."
Bobby:	"Why you always pickin' on me? Guess you be happy now. They goin kick me outa school."

Revised from: *English for Your Success*

Exactly What this Episode Illustrates

The teacher was trying to make the Black Language (BL) fit into the Mainstream American English (MAE). There was no "communication" going on between the teacher and the student. This is a "problem" that has to be worked out if there is going to be any resolution to this grave problem. This is at the heart and soul of the dysfunctional educational system that is in charge of the education of the BLO speakers and nobody seems to understand or care to correct the problem. Do Jesse Jackson and his accomplices understand the true dynamics of the "problem?"

Results of School Where Students Speak BLO (Black Language Only)

The results are dismal. We have a "pipeline to prison" system thriving. Dropout rates are very high. Graduation rates are very low. The schools will not teach BLO students English as a Second Language and as you can see "correcting" one language with another is not working.

What is the Reason behind Ignoring the Fact that BLO Students Need ESOL?

Not knowing the facts about the true "history" of Black people is the culprit. The Oakland case makes it evident that this is possible with Black people as well as White people. Why would Jesse Jackson fight on the side of Ed Koch to deny something that would be essential to improve the chances of poor Black children learning mainstream American English so that they can participate?

Well, the first and obvious answer is how powerful **THE MEDIA** *is in this country.*

Why would this country believe that the Oakland School Board wanted to use federal funds (ESOL) to teach Black English Only speakers how to speak Black English?

Race-ism Comes into the Discussion that Might Have Muddied the Water

Again White people do not know about Black people and the language we speak is one of those examples. Whites find it hard to call what Black people speak, a "language." The belief is that what Blacks speak is "incorrect English," and Blacks just need to study "regular English" and all will be well.

So the concept of having Black people taught "English, as a Second Language" means that you are calling what they presently speak, "a language," their first or native language. That seems to be a concept that the school system finds hard to embrace.

But you cannot correct Black Language into Mainstream American English. They are totally different. According to Noma LeMoine in **English** *for Your Success: A Language Development Program for African American Children, Grades Pre K-8 .*

We who speak both languages (or try to) understand this phenomenon. For example, President Obama speaks both and knows when to switch. When he visited a popular "soul food restaurant" in D.C. after moving there said this when the cashier reminded him that he had left his change: "We skrait!"

National Public Radio (NPR) even did a show on this. Then the President is able to switch to Harvard Law Review English-speak and it's so cute and worthy of discussion.

Who cares that those kids in the D.C. schools who speak BLO, are subjected to an educational system that speaks at them in MAE and blame the family for the fact that the students are not successful or "engaged" in school work?

The True Language Debate and the Impact on the Education on Urban Black Students

*I found a book recently that gives the complete "irrational and racist discourse that followed the school board's approval of the Ebonics Resolution." It covers the educational, political and linguistic issues that are embedded in the resolution. It is time for a much-needed forum for a discussion of these issues and the information in **The Real Ebonics Debate: Power, Language, and the Education of African-American Children** Edited by Theresa Perry and Lisa Delpit.*

Is there anybody who is going to open this discussion?

Does Jesse Jackson know what happened, does he know that he did not understand correctly the intent of the Oakland School Board? Does he know the grave impact and consequences of his actions in this case?

There is Precedence to Making the School System Do Something About BLO Students:

Case Name: Martin Luther King Junior Elementary School Children v. Ann Arbor School District Board 463 F. Supp. 1027

Plaintiff: Martin Luther King Junior Elementary School Children

Defendant: Ann Arbor School District Board

Location; Ann Arbor, Michigan

Year: July 12, 1979

Significant Points: It was alleged that the children speak a version of "Black English," "Black vernacular" or "Black dialect" as their home and community language that impedes their equal participation in the instructional programs, and that the school has not taken appropriate action to overcome the barrier. This case was not an effort on the part of the plaintiffs to require that they be taught "Black English" or that their instruction throughout their schooling be in "Black English," or that a dual language program be provided.

It was a straightforward effort to require the court to intervene on the children's behalf to require the Ann Arbor School District Board to take appropriate action to teach them to read in the standard English of the school, the commercial world, the arts, science and professions. This action was a cry for judicial help in opening the doors to the establishment. It was an action to keep another generation from becoming functionally illiterate.

The court required that the Board take "appropriate action" to overcome language barriers which impede equal participation in instructional programs. The court found that a language barrier exists which impedes the teachers' attempts to teach reading of standard English to students who speak "black English" in their homes. Therefore, directed the School District Board to provide a plan that the Board considers "appropriate action." Since the language barrier was found to be a barrier on the part of the teachers, the court suggested that the plan should be directed at assisting the teacher.

Does everybody get it that the American education/school system is really really bad...

Lesson #6 – Facts To Be Verified by Independent Investigation

1. What is the "history" of the Black Language; is it a language and if it is not, how do you assure that speakers of BLO get the opportunity to be taught the "language of school" so that they can participate in the American school system?

2. How did it happen that Jesse Jackson, Kwesi Mfume and Maya Angelou join with William Bennett, George Will and Rush Limbaugh to take aim at the Oakland decision?

3. Why does the school system ignore the "way the children and their parents speak" as a reason for the low performance in Title 1/No Child Left Behind schools in urban and rural areas?

4. If a child comes from a family where education has never been the focus or has never been used to escape poverty, and mainstream American English is considered speaking "White" because they don't see Blacks who speak that way and they don't watch tv shows that talk that way, is it the responsibility of the child and the family to "correct the situation" like Bill Cosby says?"

5. Why do some Blacks who were educated before Brown vs. the Board of Education and Civil Rights Movement speak "both" languages, Black Language and Mainstream American Language and those educated after that period tend to speak one or the other?

6. Should the BLO population be given an educational curriculum that allows them to receive an education and seek the American Dream like during the days before Brown vs. the Board of Education/Civil Rights Movement or let them kill themselves, be a drain on the hardworking taxpaying group and threaten the well-being of the American society?

7. Do the teachers in the Title 1/No Child Left Behind low-performing schools understand that their students are no

longer dispensable, that their "social security" benefits depend on the earning incomes of the upcoming workers?

8. Do White people who think that there children are doing well because they score better than the Black students understand that that's just like saying your children are doing better than Japanese children having their instruction in English and they have never been in ESOL classes and had no clue that there was anything wrong or that they should "protest" or try to learn the language on their own?

9. Does the NAACP have "a case" on behalf of BLO speaking students to fight for the right to an education based on the Ann Arbor Case in 1979?

10. What do linguistics say about the issue of Black Language and how to approach a positive resolution?

Letter #7 – The "Gap" that really needs our attention!

Dear Friend,

The achievement gap between Black students and White students is the latest "crisis" in American education. Not the gap between Asian students and White students and definitely not the gap between American students and the thirty countries that score ahead of our students.

As a friend, I have to tell you once again, "race-ism" is blinding America to what the real problem is in our educational system.

By now you should be a little suspect yourself about the real gap and what we really need to be doing to remove the "gap" that is going to destroy our future if we don't get it right!

Well, let's take a look at this "gap"…

Ms. Johnnie

Lesson # 7

The Achievement Gap
CODE: "We are Still Superior and They are Still Inferior"

This is the crux of the issue that "race-ism fails" America. As long as Whites are doing better than Blacks then it is hard or up to this point "impossible" to get Whites or Blacks to believe that the "gap" between the academic achievement of Whites and Blacks is irrelevant at this point in time. The "gap" that we need to be concerned about is not the gap between Blacks and Whites.

In the world of public education or education in general, there is a great deal of concern and efforts directed toward addressing and improving the "gap". Why is America fixated on the "gap"?

Let's follow the history of Blacks in America to help us understand how "racism" has distorted our rational response to real "gaps" as opposed to gaps that we have been conditioned to give a distorted view of how we are doing, and what we need to do.

If Reconstruction taught Blacks any lesson, it was that southern Whites feared Black success far more than Black failure. The more Blacks succeeded, the more they gave any indication of learning, the more they demonstrated a capability of moving out of their place, the more likely they were to arouse White resentment as hostility.

"There was one thing," W. E. B. Dubois would write, "that the White South feared more than Negro dishonesty, ignorance, and incompetency, and that was Negro honesty, knowledge and efficiency."

- Litwack, Leon F. "The Ordeal of Black Freedom." In the Southern Enigma: Essays on Race, Class and Folk Culture edited by Walter J. Fraser, Jr. and Winfred B. Moore, Jr. Westport, Conn.: Greenwood Press, 1983, pp. 5-21

"The past is never dead, It's not even past."
-As William Faulkner observed about the past

In America, in a way, the Negro tells us where the bottom is: because he is there and where he is, beneath us, we know where the limits are and how far we must not fall. We must not fall beneath him. We must never allow ourselves to fall that low...

Poor Whites particularly for whom skin color provided their only source of social status tend to cling to "the gap."

The public perception of African Americans as inferior and venal beings provides the basis of acceptability for the most outrageous of lies.

Black people are the magical faces at the bottom of society's well. Even the poorest Whites, those who must live their lives only a few levels above, gain their self-esteem by gazing down on us. Surely, they must know that their deliverance depends on letting down their ropes. Only by working together is escape possible. Over time, many reach out, but most simply watch, mesmerized into maintaining their unspoken commitment to keeping us where we are, at whatever cost to them or to us.

It is Important to remember that the great majority of Blacks moved from slavery to freedom w/no money or capital, and with nothing marketable except strong backs and hard-working hands. The only work most of them knew was farming. Moreover, they had been kept illiterate by their former masters and for the most part had been denied managerial and supervisory experience. Their entire lives had been spent taking orders from their owners and living in an environment of restrictions and controls.

- Fite, Gilbert C. Cotton Fields No More: Southern Agriculture 186501980. Lexington: University Press of Kentucky, 1984, pp. 1-29

In **Dusk of Dawn**, W.E.B. Dubois warned his people that they faced not simply "the rational, conscious determination of White folk to oppress us" but *"age-long complexes sunk now largely to unconscious habit and irrational urge."*

Carter, Dan T. Scottsboro: *A Tragedy of the American South*. Rev. ed. Baton Rouge: Louisiana State University Press, 1979., pp. 104-106.

Now, many of our youngsters feel that they are inferior from birth. Unlike children of past eras, they lack the protection of segregated institutions which, despite limitations, nonetheless provided them with a nurturing environment that insulated against attacks by outside forces. In this new, multicultural society, their question to us is: "Is the White man right? Is IQ the reason we aren't doing as well in school – that Whites always seem to excel in math while we do better in sports and music? They want to know why so many of them are killing each other, too. Is something wrong with them?

Black children are being left at the mercy of an onslaught on the very dignity of who they are, what they could become and how they were created. Many wonder how they will ever make it if they are born with a 15-point handicap. Right now, our own psyche is so delicate that when racist shots are fired by the likes of Murray and Herrnstein, most of us want to duck. But we can't. The potential for harm – direct and indirect – to the self-image of our children is incalculable. The policy implications are even more deadly.

The authors recommend radical reform of government programs, including the academic and employment quota systems supported by affirmative action. They would place greater emphasis on standardized testing as a basis for restricting opportunity. They argue that major standardized tests used to help make school and job decisions do not under-predict Black performance, but actually predict Black performance, and that standardized tests such as the SAT simply prove many Black students lack the ability to keep up academically.

They would eliminate much of the government money spent on educational programs as simply a waste – helping only the nation's bloated educational bureaucracies. Many observers agree that the policies Murray and Herrnstein recommend would reverse the 20-year effort to recruit more Black students for elite colleges and universities.

– Nat Irvin, II, Vice Chancellor for Development and University Relations, Winston Salem State University, *Black Issues in Higher Education*, November 3, 1994.

To accomplish acceptance of "inferiority" by Blacks, some of the following have been used:

- limit his horizons
- restrict knowledge of the world
- smother his hope for better things
- degrade his image of himself and his people

In South Carolina where I know the most about, the brainwashing of Black Carolinians to believe in his own inferiority and to convince him that White supremacy was "natural" to endure this belief he was to be made so hopeless and helpless he would resign himself to White domination.

The case now is that White America has become so obsessed with being better than Blacks that the "gap" that is really significant and worthy of concern is that the gap in national incomes is approaching a crisis as those in the top fifth now earn more than their counterparts in the bottom four fifths combined.

A different but no less disturbing comparison: the top two million income earners in this country earn more than the next one hundred million.

So when the Post and Courier ran a series of articles on the "poor state of education" for the poor at-risk group, I sent this email to a colleague who I was trying to "un-condition" regarding who's at risk and who's really at-risk:

Dear _____,

Will the Post and Courier or any of its readers show any concern for or about our smartest and brightest?

The school district is always able to get off the hook when "poor, one-parent, free lunch, no parental involvement, achievement-gapped children" aren't successful. (They say it's not their fault, it's the children's, their parents and their circumstances that is the problem)

And they have had a free ride since A Nation at Risk, 1983 came out and the "reforms" began.

Well, does anybody care that the students at Academic Magnet have the right parents, the right income, the right culture, and in one year the school has gone from #7 to #12, and has been kicked off the Top Ten List of Best High Schools in US News...

And has anybody checked to see where the Top Ten students place among the international comparisons? or care?

When will the parents of Academic Magnet read *A Nation at Risk, 1983*, and understand that that report was about their kids? Their kids are the "at-risk" kids; that's how "conditioned" the school system is, they picked the "poor, one-parent, free lunch, etc. kids as the at-risk group and gets all the money and attention."

Does anybody care that "ignorance" is consuming us and we still have our chests stuck out with pride because there is still the "gap"?

-Johnnie Mitchell

James P. Comer in "No Need to Wait for a Miracle- A Successful Education Program is Exploding the Myth That Black Low-Income Urban Youth Can't Achieve Excellence in Public Schools" sums up this idea that there is no interest in Black success. Have you heard about Dr. Comer's success with urban Black youth? Has his program been embraced to remove "the gap"?

Maybe I've missed something, what is the value of closing the achievement gap between "Black" students and "White" students?

Lesson # 7 – Facts to be Independently Investigated

1. Is the "academic gap" between Blacks and Whites more important than the "gap" between the highest possible score on the SAT and the #12 best high school (2400/1800)?

2. Is the achievement gap between Blacks and Whites more important than the gap between America and 30 other countries?

3. What is America doing about the Black/White gap?

4. What are the schools successfully closing the Black and White doing differently from the schools that are unsuccessful?

5. Could the testing companies "re-calibrate" the normal bell curve scoring and close the gap?

6. Do the President's daughters' scores reflect the "gap?" (we'll never know but he and his family will)

Letter #8 – Our Education System 25 Years After *"A Nation at Risk, 1983"*

Dear Friend,

I watch CNN and MSNBC, I read the newspaper daily and I get the important news of the day when I check my email every day.

I might have missed it but I didn't see the 25th Anniversary of A Nation at Risk, 1983 get any coverage.

That makes me very sad and scared. To hear the "conservatives" in this country young and old worry about the "debt" that the next generation will have to bear if we add to the deficit makes me cringe. This is how I interpret the "crisis" we are in right now. If our house is on fire and water is available to save the house, I don't think this is the time to "conserve" water and let the house burn down. (So we now have saved water but we don't have a house)

That's how I look at our condition in America right now if we don't "save" the country, the "debt" will be irrelevant.

Right now I feel like the house has burned down even though we were given adequate warning 25 years ago but because we mis-interpreted the warning, the "house burned down" and we are wandering in the "wilderness" with the Democrats scrambling to "re-construct a house" and the conservatives' concern is on the "cost to the next generation."

Did we miss some things? Well, I think we missed some things because of the "conditioning of race-ism" kept us from recognizing and valuing the "warnings!"

Lovers of this country who are on this journey with me to see if we can "de-program" ourselves, rest assured that your Guide was diligent and did get a copy of the report on the 25th Anniversary of A Nation at Risk, 2008. In this Lesson we will look back at the 1983 report and the results of the "reforms" that took place during that 25 year period.

Let's continue to investigate the programming of "race-ism." This time we have facts/numbers and "liars may figure, but figures don't lie" and these figures have not been subjected to the "normal bell curve" manipulation of statistics (where "liars" are sometimes given a wink and a nod).

You be the judge…

Ms. Johnnie

SECTION 4
THE FAILING OF AMERICA

Lesson # 8

A Stagnant Nation:
Why American Students Are *Still* at Risk, 2008

(25th Anniversary of A Nation-At-Risk, 1983)

Well, twenty-five years later let's look at the results of the "reform" following the WARNING in 1983.

You have probably not seen or heard of the findings. I thank the "Universe" for making it available to me. I was going along like everybody else, not waiting or seeking out the twenty-five year report on the 1983 A Nation-at-Risk.

We had in essence declared war on ourselves by having a school system that was so bad it would be considered a declaration of war if it had been inflicted on us a foreign source.

As you will recall, the American education/school system was "the enemy" that was allowed to determine who and how to address the issues in the report. The school system in their wisdom, of course, did not find that the report was about them in anyway, so they had to search for a target for "reform." That target turned out to be the "poor Black at-risk population."

Reading this report of the findings on the 25 year reform would be hilarious if it wasn't so sad…

A Stagnant Nation: Why American Students Are Still at Risk, 2008

Twenty-five years ago, the National Commission on Excellence in Education released *A Nation at Risk* to thunderous publicity. While the national conversation about education would never be the same, stunningly few of the Commission's recommendations actually have been enacted.

Key recommendations related to time, teaching, and standards have yet to be realized. For example, regarding Standards and Expectations:

The Commission recommended that states and districts raise standards and expectations and said that classroom grades should reflect actual learning. Yet 12th grade test scores in reading and science actually *dropped* at the same time that average high school GPAs skyrocketed. Students are earning better grades in "tougher" courses, yet actual learning is either stagnant or in decline. At the same time, states have failed to set rigorous academic standards in the lower grades. One study found that out of 32 states, *none* had set performance benchmarks for 4th grade reading that were high enough to meet the proficient level on the National Assessment of Educational Progress (NAEP). Twenty-four had set them so low that they did not reach *even the most basic level.*

As a result, learning has not improved much, either. Elementary and middle school students have made some gains over the past quarter century, but high school achievement has declined or remained stagnant. Recent 12th grade assessment results reveal the same woeful level of preparation *A Nation at Risk* lamented in 1983. One in four high school seniors cannot glean basic information about subway fares by reading a Metrorail guide. Nearly half can't answer a simple multiple choice question about the function of a neuron, and three out of four can't describe wind and rain as two ways that rocks can be broken down by the weather. In math, two out of five high school seniors lack skills that are commonly taught in 7th or 8th grade and are necessary to learn trades that do not require a college degree.

Meanwhile, the United States has fallen even farther behind as other countries make concerted efforts to improve their education systems. America once had the best high school graduation rate, but it has now fallen to 21st among industrialized nations. Our college-attainment rate plummeted from second in 1995 to 14th just a decade later. America's 15-year-olds perform below average in math, science, and problem-solving. Even our best students can no longer compete. In math, America has a below average proportion of top performers; our best math students rank 24th when compared with top performers in 29 other countries.

After 25 years, time is running out on American's opportunity to enact a robust national education reform agenda. We cannot afford to fail in our mission to provide students with a world-class education. We cannot afford to graduate millions of high school seniors who lack skills in reading and math that they should have learned in middle school. We especially cannot afford to continue slipping farther and farther behind the other nations of the world. Our students deserve better, and our nation's economic security is at greater risk now that ever before.

Introduction

Nearly 90 million schoolchildren have entered 1st grade since the National Commission on Excellence in Education released *A Nation at Risk* a quarter of a century ago. Our leaders have failed nearly all of those children. In fact, America's students have been doubly betrayed – first by the *educational* failure described in *A Nation at Risk* and then by the *political* failure to fix those problems.

When Secretary of Education Terrel H. Bell appointed the Commission in 1981, it was amid media accounts of declining academic standards in American schools. The problem had taken root over the course of several decades.

Based largely on those trends, the Commission famously warned of "a rising tide of mediocrity" in American education, one that ultimately would undermine the nation's economic security.

No education report before or since has had a greater impact on the national debate about American's schools. *A Nation at Risk* generated tremendous publicity, ended the complacency that was fueling low educational expectations, and launched the modern "school reform" movement. Yet today, as the world continues to change rapidly and demand for skilled workers accelerates, America's economic future remains gravely at risk because we have not implemented the Commission's full set of recommendations to provide students with a truly world-class education system.

Even the students who managed to graduate from our K-12 schools ready for college and work have been robbed. Stanford economist Eric Hanushek has calculated that, "had we undertaken policies after *A Nation at Risk* that truly reformed our schools, we could today be enjoying substantially higher national income. Indeed, direct estimates of the lost opportunities suggest we could today pay for the entire budget for K-12 education from the dividends of effective reform."

Stalled Out: Little or No Progress on Educational Outcomes

A Nation at Risk decried the poor academic preparation America's high school students. But more than two decades later, the knowledge and skills of our high school students remain nearly the same or, in some cases, have become even worse.

In the early 1990s, the Department of Education developed a parallel NAEP test in order to administer more "modern" assessments to complement the long-term test, which must remain unchanged to provide stable comparisons to the 1970s. The latest results for 12th graders on that newer NAEP assessment reveal a disturbing trend: Twelfth grade reading scores have *declined* significantly since the assessment was first given in 1992. Reading skills are declining for students from all backgrounds, including those with college-educated parents.

Overall, the proportion of 12th graders reading at a proficient level dropped from an already low 40 percent in 1992 to just 35 percent in 2005, and the percentage scoring at even the most basic level slipped from 80 to 73. By 2005, nearly one in four high school seniors could not glean basic information about subway fares by reading a Metrorail guide.

The poor performance has devastating consequences for our young people and our economy.

What would the Commission members who wrote *A Nation at Risk* have thought if they could have foreseen that a quarter century later, two out of five high school seniors would lack math skills commonly taught in 7th or 8th grade and necessary to learn trades that do not require a college degree?

Even more distressing, reading is not the only subject in which our high school seniors are getting worse. The percentage of 12th graders scoring proficient in science dropped from 21 percent in 1996 to 18 percent in 2005. Scores are declining in all the sciences –earth, physical, and biological-precisely at a time when Americans must confront urgent environmental problems and complex ethical questions related to new technologies. Nearly half of America's high school seniors could not answer a simple multiple choice question about the function of a neuron. Three out of four could not list wind and rain as two ways that rocks can be broken down by the weather.

Average Mathematics Scores of 15-year-old Students by Country (2006)

Rank	Country	Score
1	Finland	548
2	Korea	547
3	Netherlands	531

4	Switzerland	530
5	Canada	527
6	Japan	523
7	New Zealand	522
8	Australia	520
9	Belgium	520
10	Denmark	520
11	Czech Republic	510
12	Iceland	506
13	Austria	505
14	Germany	504
15	Sweden	502
16	Ireland	501
17	France	496
18	Poland	495
19	United Kingdom	495
20	Slovak Republic	492
21	Hungary	491
22	Luxembourg	490
23	Spain	480
25	**United States**	**474**
26	Portugal	466
27	Italy	462
28	Greece	459
29	Turkey	424
30	Mexico	406
(31)	**U.S.**	**(?)**

-(according to Sec. of Ed. Arne Duncan-2009)

"Top U.S. students are outperformed just like average and struggling US students. [...] The United States does not just have more students performing badly-it also has many fewer students performing well."

Paralysis: Why Achievement Is Stalled and Our Position Eroding

Why have we stood still while other countries advanced? After all, *A Nation at Risk* prompted a torrent of proposals, speeches, events, and papers at the state and local levels. In reality, however, all of that talk and activity ultimately amounted to very little real change in the way we operate our education system.

What follows is one possibility of why America has gone in the wrong direction while other countries are moving forward:

This is the Executive Summary of a report, "Benchmarking for Success: Ensuring U.S. Students Receive a World-Class Education:

Around the globe, governments are eagerly comparing their educational outcomes to the best in the world. The goal is not just to see how they rank, but rather to identify and learn from top performers and rapid improvers –from nations and states that offer ideas for boosting their own performance. This process, known as "international benchmarking," has become a critical tool for governments striving to create world-class education systems.

In American education, "benchmarking" often simply means comparing performance outcomes or setting performance targets (or "benchmarks"). But in business and among education leaders in other countries, it means much more. The American Productivity and Quality Center puts it this way: "Benchmarking is the practice of being humble enough to admit that someone else has a better process and wise enough to learn how to match or even surpass them."

Countries and states have good reason to make the effort. Technological, economic, and political trends have combined to increase demand for higher skills while heightening competition for quality jobs. Rule-bound jobs on factory floors and in offices are being automated and outsourced. The world's knowledge-and innovation economy favors workers who have postsecondary education or training, strong fundamental skills in math and reading, and the ability to solve unfamiliar problems and communicate effectively.

At the same time, new technologies and corporate strategies have opened the global labor market to billions of people from places like Eastern Europe, India, China, and Brazil which had been left out. An increasing variety of work tasks can be digitized and performed nearly anywhere in the world. More jobs are going to the best educated no matter where they live, which means that Americans will face more competition than ever at work.

International trade agreements, such as China's membership in the World Trade Organization in 2001, have hastened this transformation. Since 1980, global trade has grown 2.5 times faster than the global gross domestic product (GDP). Recent estimates put today's world exports at $12.5 trillion, nearly 20 percent of world GDP.

The global economy is here to stay, with recent research suggesting that it is evolving and its impact intensifying at a stunning pace. "Globalization is happening faster than people think," says Vivek Wadhwa, Wertheim Fellow at Harvard Law School's Labor and Worldlife program and Duke University Executive in Residence. His recent research shows that companies are no longer just outsourcing production but are farming out innovation as well. "Having India and China conduct such sophisticated research and participate in drug discovery was unimaginable even five years ago," he says.

Education is a tremendously important lever for ensuring competitiveness and prosperity in the age of globalization, albeit not the only one. Recent economic studies show that high skills lead to better wages, more equitable distributions of income, and substantial gains in economic productivity. Higher math performance at the end of high school translates into a 12 percent increase in future earnings. If the United

States raised students' math and science skills to globally competitive levels over the next two decades, its GDP would be an additional 36 percent higher 75 years from now.

The race is on among nations to create knowledge-fueled innovation economies. In Singapore, Germany, China, Brazil, Korea, and other countries around the world, educational improvement is viewed as a critical part of that mission. Nations and states are therefore working hard to benchmark their education systems to establish a solid foundation for economic development in the 21st century. Some are finding innovative ways to measure their students' progress internationally. Others are examining high-performing and fast-improving nations to learn about best practices that they then adapt or adopt to improve their own systems.

American education has not adequately responded to these new challenges. The United States is falling behind other countries in the resource that matters most in the new global economy: human capital. American 15 –year-olds ranked 25th in math and 21st in science achievement on the most recent international assessment conducted in 2006. (31st in 2009 according to Secretary of Education Arne Duncan) At the same time, the U. S. ranked high in inequity, with the third largest gap in science scores between students from different socioeconomic groups.

The U.S. is rapidly losing its historic edge in educational attainment as well. As recently as 1995, America still tied for first in college and university graduation rates, but by 2006 had dropped to 14th. That same year it had the second-highest college dropout rate of 27 countries.

State leaders already are deeply engaged in efforts to raise standards, advance teaching quality, and improve low-performing schools. International benchmarking provides an additional tool for making that process more effective, offering insights and ideas that cannot be garnered solely from looking within and across state lines. To that end, the partner organizations and International Benchmarking Advisory Group call on state leaders to take the following actions:

Action 1: Upgrade state standards by adopting a common core of internationally benchmarked standards in math and language arts for grades K-12 to ensure that students are equipped with the necessary knowledge and skills to be globally competitive.

Action 2: Leverage states' collective influence to ensure that textbooks, digital media, curricula, and assessments are aligned to internationally benchmarked standards and draw on lessons from high-performing nations and states.

Action 3: Revise state policies for recruiting, preparing, developing, and supporting teachers and school leaders to reflect the human capital practices of top-performing nations and states around the world.

Action 4: Hold schools and systems accountable through monitoring, interventions, and support to ensure consistently high performance, drawing upon international best practices.

Action 5: Measure state-level education performance globally by examining student achievement and attainment in an international context to ensure that, over time, students are receiving the education they need to compete in the 21st century economy.

State leaders also should tackle "the equity imperative" by creating strategies for closing the achievement gap between students from different racial and socioeconomic backgrounds in each of the action steps above. Reducing inequality in education is not only socially just, it's essential for ensuring that the United States retain a competitive edge.

Research shows that education systems in the United States tend to give disadvantaged and low-achieving students a watered down curriculum and place them in larger classes taught by less qualified

teachers- exactly opposite of the educational practices of high-performing countries.

Nations around the world are facing a new education imperative, and many are seizing the historical moment to provide their citizens with better opportunities and stronger economies.

America must seize this moment too, with states leading the way.

For Andreas Schleicher, head of the Indicators and Analysis Division at the Organisation for Economic Co-Operation and Development's Directorate for Education, the case for adopting a global view to improving education is undeniable:

It is only through such benchmarking that countries can understand relative strengths and weaknesses of their education system and identify best practices and ways forward. The world is indifferent to tradition and past reputations, unforgiving of frailty and ignorant of custom or practice, Success will go to those individuals and countries which are swift to adapt, slow to complain, and open to change.

In conclusion, other nations have benefited from America's historic example by expanding educational opportunities for their own citizens. Now it is time for U.S. leaders to ensure that Americans develop the skills they need to compete-and help the U.S. remain competitive-in a rapidly changing world.

The federal government can help, but states must lead. They must look beyond their borders and America's shores to fully understand how to benchmark expectations for student learning. They must significantly broaden the policy lens by drawing lessons from the highest performing most equitable and fastest advancing nations and states around the globe and adapting the very best educational practices to incorporate here at home.

If states in other countries can shape the response to the global education imperative, states in America must do so as well. And state leaders have both the authority and an obligation to ensure that students attend globally competitive schools and school districts. America cannot maintain its place in the world-economically, socially, or culturally-unless all of its students gain the skills that allow them to compete on a global scale. The United States will only achieve true international competitiveness when state education policies and institutions are restructured to meet 21st century realities.

Warnings from Horace Mann in 1846:

They, then, who knowingly withhold sustenance from a newborn child, and he dies, are guilty of infanticide. And, by the same reasoning, they who refuse to enlighten the intellect of a rising generation are guilty of degrading the human race! They who refuse to train up children in the way they should go, are training up incendiaries and madmen to destroy property and life, and to invade and pollute the sanctuaries of society.

It's the school system!

It's the worst place in the world for our students to spend any time! Everybody hates being there or being a part of the system, the students, teachers, the administrators, the parents. Everybody in the school system hates the school system but the public protects and defends it like the school system is "sacred." The public wants to blame and put the responsibility on anything and anybody but the school system! The students aren't doing well because of the society, the parents, the economy, the lack of parental involvement, the marital status of the parents, the list goes on and on and on.

Has anybody looked at what goes on in America's schools, colleges and universities? That system will turn wonderful children into the children we have today. If you throw garbage on children, they will eventually think that's what they are!

Are you all with me?

Let's move on…

Lesson # 8 – Facts To Be Verified by Independent Investigation

1. Are 15 year olds truly scoring #31 compared to other countries in the world?

2. Do we have the best educational system in the world?

3. Is there a problem/conflict between believing you have the #1 educational system but you produce a product that is #31 in the world?

4. Do you think A Nation at Risk was addressing the status of poor Black children? Or the entire educational system which is predominantly White?

5. Why do you think after 25 years things in education have gotten much worst, the warnings in 1983 have come true and the 25th report did not become a topic of interest to the Media?

6. Are White students doing fine and Black students are doing poorly?

7. Do you think there is a relationship between "education" and our "economy?"

8. How is the "normal bell curve" and "race" used in the international testing?

9. If a poor Black woman has some good ideas about improving our educational system, would you be interested in investigating her ideas?

10. Does "race" have anything to do with education in America?

Letter # 9 – Is this "Race Concept" Working For Us?

Dear Comrades,

I feel like we are now closer that friends, we are now comrades, fighting to learn how we can help our country, ourselves and our future.

I tell you this country is DIVIDED. As a Black person I see things that some Whites and some Blacks don't. It's like this "I see dead people." While others think that America is one country and the division of "race-ism" is behind us, "I see 'RACE-ISM'" and it's alive and well! If I can only help you to believe me!

That's what I've been trying to do!

My girlfriend tells me it's like an abusive relationship and the abuser doesn't perceive the situation the way an outside party may see it. When Michelle Obama made that statement that she was proud of her country for the first time, "we" made her "eat" those words! I know what she meant and she was absolutely correct the first time, but the country didn't "see" it that way and she was made to see it the "right" way or pay the consequences (not be First Lady, not be valued and face the wrath of the abuser!) She made a choice and decided to "say the right thing" and have her abuser reward her with the White House.

I believe that without the mentoring of the Rev. Jeremiah Wright there would be no "President Barack Obama." What President Barack Obama did by running and winning is the most "militant" act ever successfully executed by a Black person in America!

I think we are ready to believe a Black woman who "sees 'race-ism' [dead people] and can help us restart education in a non-racial America for a smart and successful country for us and our children and grandchildren.

Is the "divided America" working for us? While you may think we are not divided, please believe me, there is another perspective!

Let's continue, my comrades…

-Ms. Johnnie

Lesson #9

Collapse of a Divided America

-A House Divided Cannot Stand-
"Race" Fails America

Justice Thurgood Marshall – receiving the Liberty Bell Award shortly before his death, 7/4/92

I wish I could say that racism and prejudice were only distant memories... and that liberty and equality were just around the bend. I wish I could say that America has come to appreciate diversity and to see and accept similarity. But as I look around, I see not a nation of unity but of division – Afro and White, indigenous and immigrant, rich and poor, educated and illiterate... But there is a price to be paid for division and isolation.

We cannot play ostrich. Democracy cannot flourish amid fear. Liberty cannot bloom amid hate. Justice cannot take root amid rage. We must go against the prevailing wind. We must dissent from the indifference. We must dissent from the apathy. We must dissent from the fear, the hatred and the mistrust. We must dissent from a government that has left its young without jobs, education or hope. We must dissent from the poverty of vision and the absence of moral leadership. We must dissent because America has no choice but to do better.

... Take a chance, won't you? Knock down the fences that divide. Tear apart the walls that imprison. Reach out; freedom lies just on the other side.

Again, Horace Mann, 1846 says:

They, then, who knowingly withhold sustenance from a newborn child, and he dies, are guilty of infanticide. And, by the same reasoning, they who refuse to enlighten the intellect of a rising generation, are guilty of degrading the human race! They, who refuse to train up children in the way they should go, are training up incendiaries and madmen to destroy property and life, and to invade and pollute the sanctuaries of society.

By now, many people are familiar with America's poor academic performance on the international stage. Forty years ago, the United States had the highest high school completion rate in the world. Today, it ranks 18th out of 24 industrialized nations. In 1995, the rate of Americans going to college was among the highest in the world. Since then, 13 other countries boast higher college graduation rates than the United States. What can the United States learn from countries that seem to be doing a better job of preparing students for the 21st –century economy?

-Group Offer Ways to Improve U. S. Education by Eddy Ramirez, *U.S. News & World Report (from Yahoo! News)*

Medical insurance is out of reach for 46 million of Americans. Our country is at war in Afghanistan and Iraq as well as with a ghostly omnipresent foe known as terrorism. Our national debt is stupendous, our stock market has plunged and many companies once thought to be towers of strength have failed.

What's "Race" got to do with it?

What started out with Black, White, Yellow and Red is now "say what?"

And we all know it was really about Black and White [owner and slave; superior/inferior]

Now it's:

White, non-Hispanic
Hispanic or Latino
Black/African descent
Asian
Korean
Japanese
Chinese
Indian
Arab
Native American
Alaska Native
Native Hawaiian
Arabic/Middle Eastern
Italian
Jewish
Mixed Race
Pacific Islander
Russian

How many of you have heard that split hair doesn't or can't grow? We are so busy trying to keep up with the splits that we are not improving; we have fallen off the cliff and don't know what to do...
Racism is a luxury we can no longer afford.
Everybody needs to be well educated and perform to their maximum to restore and sustain America's economic vitality.

I never thought the bombs of "race-ism" would be detonated this way. No need for apology, reparation isn't an issue, there is no hate, let's do what we've got to do for our survival. It's not survival of the fittest; it's survival of the smart!
It's time to restart education in a Non-Racial America where we can all be winners!
Teaching and Learning for ALL must become the manta!

Lesson #9 – Facts to be Verified by Individual Investigation

1. Is America where you want it to be?

2. Does it matter that Whites are doing better than Blacks?

3. Is it helping anybody that Whites score higher on "normal bell curve" standardized tests than Blacks?

4. Would it serve everybody to have Black students and White students engaged in a vigorous competition against the World rather than stagnation between each other?

5. Is it better for our welfare to have Black students get a good education or is it better for us to have students outside of this country get a good education?

6. If Blacks could learn well before Brown vs. the Board of Education dismantled the Black school system, what is different now that they are in a White school system, why can't they learn anymore?

7. Why do some schools in America (outside of the South) close the achievement gap between Blacks and Whites but there are none in South Carolina?

8. Is an education more impactful on a Black person than a White person?

9. What makes a Black person Black and a White person White?

10. What is the difference between Black America and White America; is it due to "nature" or "circumstances?"

Letter #10 – Can We Give Up "Race" and Become One People?

Dear Partner,

For whatever reason, can we be one? If you buy into the theory that there is only one race and it's time to get over the division, that's terrific! If you still believe that we are of "different races," are you practical and pragmatic enough to still agree that it is in everybody's best interest to "UNITE" and become ONE?

Our "failure" has united us whether we accept one reason or another!

Those of you who are waiting for America to get back to where it was pre-economic meltdown, I hope you are right! For those of you who understand that we fell off a cliff I really don't believe we are ever going to put "humpty-dumpty" back together again!

However, with "education" we can "reconstruct" a new America, a smart America where rewards are given to the hardest working students; not "preference" that rewards "mediocrity?"

A great educational system will "reconstruct" a great America. I know what a "good education" can do. Blacks used education to reach the highest office in the land. At the end of the Civil War with no forty acres and a mule, Blacks went from not owning anything, not even themselves to achieve enormously in a "foreign" and sometimes "hostile" environment.

I think we face that challenging opportunity again and together we can do this!

The work will be easy, the hard part will be the "psychological" conditioning that will have to be overcome. If the motivation is great enough, I think we will be able to come together, "restart education" and let the good times roll again!

-Ms. Johnnie

SECTION 5
THE LAW OF DIMINISHING RETURNS

Lesson #10

We Are One
Reconstruction Time!

We are one! We are Americans in trouble...

When a child enters the schools system, there is a check list (race, one or two parents, free lunch or not and "readiness" scores) and if he is considered "ready" to learn, then he gets the "in" sign; if he doesn't pass then he is "out" and is considered "not ready." Either way, written in or written out, he is "written off" in this school system!

*It is really unfortunate that "failure" is the unifying factor for us as Americans today. However, "unity" is valuable at all cost. Again, it's unfortunate that we had/have to pay such a high price for "unity." Through our "Lessons" you will recall that from the beginning we embarked on a course starting with "slavery" and "freedom" to "free **but** 'inferior'" "free **and** 'superior.'" With those divisions at the beginning of the period after the Civil War, called Reconstruction, we have been on a course of eventual destruction! There were many warnings, we ignored the signs, and now we still resist or deny the realities of our situation today.*

That is why the odds are against me getting this book into your hands, I am writing frantically to get the manuscript completed as I observe my beloved country continue to spin in a spiral of "failure" and a delusion of why and how to stop the decline.

With my passion and optimism, I write on with the belief that this book will reach your hands and you will read, understand and become a part of the "reconstruction" that can save us all!

First there was Black Reconstruction after the Civil War; then White Reconstruction until now and today we must enter RECONSTRUCTION for all, American Reconstruction...

I just saw a piece on MSNBC on the anniversary of Brown vs Board of Education where Newt Gingrich and Al Sharpton had just met with President Obama lobbying him on behalf of EDUCATION. They were both singing praises to President Obama, evoking the 1983 A Nation at Risk, *and the 50% high school graduation rate of Blacks; and the fact that 26 years after A Nation at Risk, the United States is now #25 in the world.*

Time for a RECONSTRUCTION, a truly AMERICAN RECON-STRUCTION.

What brings us together today is our predicament; let's begin the litany of what "unites" us, let the litany begin:

- **Most grown-ups flunk test of basic science, economics**

- Less than half of American adults know the Earth orbits the sun yearly, according to a basic science survey.

- Only about 25 percent of American adults got passing grades in a survey of 2,006 adults by the National Science Foundation of what people know about basic science and economics. Even fewer of those surveyed felt they were well-informed about the subjects.

- The worst showing came when those surveyed were asked to define scientific terms. Only about 9 percent knew what a molecule was, and only 21 percent could define DNA.

- In a test of environmental understanding, a third of Americans surveyed understood the effects of a thinning of the ozone layer, 14 percent could identify locations of ozone holes and 5 percent could give a scientific explanation of acid rain.

- "Only 10 percent feel very well informed about science and technology, and studies show that only a small segment of the population has a strong grasp of basic scientific ideas," according to a report…

- Despite a fundamental lack of understanding, the survey found 72 percent of American adults believe science research is worthwhile. Only 13 percent took the opposite view.

- The survey, however, found many Americans fearful of some aspects of science. Support for the nuclear power was about evenly split, with 43 percent saying its benefits were greater than its risks, and 42 percent taking an opposite view. Fourteen percent were uncertain.

- Genetic engineering fared only slightly better. Forty-three percent saw it as beneficial, but 35 percent said its dangers outweigh the benefits. About 20 percent were undecided.

This is the test that was given on basic science:

<u>THE QUIZ</u>
The quiz given by researchers from the National Science Foundation to determine how much American adults know about basic science:

1. The center of the Earth is very hot. (True or False)

2. The oxygen we breathe comes from plants. (True or False)

3. Electrons are smaller than atoms. (True or False)

4. The continents on which we live have been moving their location for millions of years and will continue to move in the future. (True or False)

5. Human beings, as we know them today, developed from earlier species of animals. (True or False)

---

6. The earliest human beings lived at the same time as the dinosaurs. (True or False)

7. Which travels faster: light or sound?

8. How long does it take for the Earth to go around the sun: one day, one month, or one year?

9. Tell me, in your own words, what is DNA?

10. Tell me, in your own words, what is a molecule?

Answers, along with the percentage who had correct responses:

1. True. 78 percent.
2. True. 85 percent.
3. True. 44 percent.
4. True. 79 percent.
5. True. 44 percent.
6. True. 44 percent.
7. Light. 75 percent.
8. One year. 47 percent.
9. DNA, or deoxyribonucleic acid, is a large molecule in the chromosomes that contains the genetic information for each cell. 21 percent.
10. Molecule is the smallest unit of a chemical compound capable of existing independently while retaining properties of the original substance. 9 percent.-*from The Charlotte Observer, by Paul Recer/Associated Press*

Nearly half of adults lacking literacy skills

Nearly half of adult Americans read and write so poorly that they are unable to function effectively in the workplace, according to a report released by the Department of Education.

Education officials stopped sort of using the word "illiterate" to describe even those at the lowest ability levels, saying many have rudimentary reading, writing and math skills.

"In many ways Americans are better educated that ever before, but the demand for skills is continuing to rise," said Deputy Education Secretary Madeline Kunin. "It's a question of keeping pace, and that's where we're not succeeding."

The 90 million people with poor literacy skills represents 47 percent of the nation's 191 million adults.

"The number is shocking but that doesn't surprise me," Education Secretary Dick Riley said after revealing the survey results.

He noted that many of those with low reading, writing and math skills also live in poverty.

The study, by the Education Department's National Center for Educational Statistics, showed that those functioning at the higher skill levels were more likely to be employed, work more weeks in a year and earn higher wages than those at the lower levels...

Participants were tested and scored in three areas: prose, document and quantitative. The prose score was based on ability to locate information in written text like newspaper articles or instructions. The document score was based on ability to locate facts in complex materials and combine it with prior knowledge to generate new information. The quantitative score was based on ability to glean mathematical information from documents.

The study, ordered by Congress, also showed that:

- As many as 40 million of the nation's 191 million adults possess the lowest level of skills, meaning they can total an entry on a bank deposit slip, locate the time or place of a meeting or form, or identify a piece of specific information in a brief news article. Many of the respondents were unable to complete even those tasks.

- Young adults – those 21 to25 years old – surveyed last year showed literacy skills 11 to 14 percentage points lower than those in the same age group participating in a 1985 survey.

The report blames the change in part on the shifting demographics of the population group, particularly the number of people speaking English as a second language.

-from The Island Packet, Thursday, September 9, 1993, Washington (AP)

A Boston article by the Associate Press:

Aspiring teachers can't pass Massachusetts test

So many aspiring educators flunked Massachusetts' first basic reading-and-writing test for teachers that officials graded them on a curve, and now some are wondering whether dumb bureaucrats are promoting dumb teachers.

The Board of Education voted this week to adjust the passing grade to reduce the number of those who failed from 56% to 44 percent – prompting outrage from acting Gov. Paul Cellucci and others.

House Speaker Thomas Finneran said he has seen the tests, which were not released, and was appalled to see candidates couldn't "define a noun or a verb or what democracy means or the meaning of the word "imminent."

-Will Moredock in the City Paper

This article presents many of the items that are at the crux of the thesis of this book.

U. S. students trail global peers in math

Americans scored below average in testing from algebra and geometry to statistics

Associated Press

Washington – Fifteen –year-olds in the United States don't have the math skills to match up to peers in many other industrialized nations, test scores released Monday show.

The latest international comparison also underscores an achievement gap in America: White U. S. students score above average, while Blacks and Hispanics scored below it.

Overall, U.S. students scored below the international average in total math literacy and in every specific area tested, from geometry and algebra to statistics and computation.

Known as the Program of International Student Assessment, the test measures math, reading and science literacy among 15-year-old students. It is given every three years.

This time, the main focus was math.

The test is not a measure of grade-level curriculum, but rather a cumulative gauge of skills learned inside and outside the classroom – and how well students apply them to real-life problems.

It also aims to give the United States an external reality check about how it is doing.

Among 29 industrialized countries, the United States scored below 20 nations and above five in math.

The U.S. performance was about the same as Poland, Hungary and Spain.

When compared with all 39 nations that produced scores, the United States was below 23 countries, above 11 and about the same as four others, with Latvia joining the middle group.

"If we want to be competitive, we have some mountains to climb," Deputy Education Secretary Eugene Hickok said at a news conference Monday.

The test is run by the Organization for Economic Cooperation and Development, a Paris-based intergovernmental group of industrialized countries.

Compared with peers from the OECD countries, even the highest U.S. achievers – those in the top percent of U.S. students – were outperformed.

Hickok cited two likely factors: insufficient qualifications and knowledge among many U.S. math teachers, and not enough effort to engage students in math at an early age.

Private researchers and the federal government will help reveal some underlying lessons for the United States by doing more analysis of the numbers, said Robert Lerner, commissioner of the Education Department's National Center for Education Statistics.

U.S. students also scored below the international average in problem-solving, a new category that tests one's ability to use skills that cut across traditional subject areas.

In the United States, 262 schools and 5,456 students took part in the tests, including representative shares of public and private schools.

Average math literacy scores of 15-year-old students in country, 2003		
Hong Kong	-	550
Finland	-	544
South Korea	-	542
Netherlands	-	538
Liechtenstein	-	536
Japan	-	534
Canada	-	533
Belgium	-	529
Switzerland	-	527
New Zealand	-	524
Australia	-	524
Czech Republic	-	517
Iceland	-	515
Denmark	-	514
France	-	511
Sweden	-	509
Austria	-	506
Ireland	-	503
Germany	-	503
Slovak Republic	-	498
Norway	-	495
Luxembourg	-	493
Poland	-	490
Hungary	-	490
Spain	-	485
Latvia	-	483
United States	-	**483**
Portugal	-	466
Italy	-	466
Greece	-	455

Turkey	-	423
Uruguay	-	422
Thailand	-	417
Mexico	-	385
Indonesia	-	360
Tunisia	-	359

America's international edge in student achievement is slipping, as other countries take education reform to heart.

Elevating Performance in a 'Flat World' by Andreas Schleicher:

Summary:

Together, skills and technology have flattened the world, such that all work that can be digitized, automatized, and outsourced can now be done by the most effective and competitive individuals or enterprises, wherever on the globe they are located.

No country has been able to capitalize on the opportunities this "flat world" provides more than the United States, which can draw on the most highly educated labor force among the principal industrialized nations, at least when measured in terms of formal qualifications.

That advantage, however, is largely a result of the "first-mover advantage," which the United States gained after World War II by massively increasing educational enrollments. It is now eroding quickly, as more and more countries reach and surpass U.S. qualification levels. In fact, many countries are now close to ensuring that virtually all young adults leave schools with at least a high school diploma, which the OECD indicators highlight as the baseline qualification for reasonable earnings and employment prospects. In contrast, the United States has stood still on this measure. Among OECD countries, only New Zealand, Spain, Turkey, and Mexico now have lower high school completion rates than the United States.

Corresponding to the sad state of America in terms of education, let's look at the status of a critical area facing America. In my estimation, this is a prime example of what happens to an "ignorant" society.

Time Magazine's front page story:

Annual Checkup: The Sorry State of American Health: Despite advances in medicine, Americans are less healthy than we used to be, and the next generation may be even worse off.

America's Health Checkup
It's hard enough to make it to your own annual physical. In this issue, Time takes the entire nation to the doctor.

By Alice Park

If you're like 67% of Americans, you're currently overweight or obese. If you're like 27%, your blood pressure is too high. If you're like a whopping 96% of the population, you may not be able to recall the last time you had a salad, since you're one of the hundreds of millions of Americans who rarely eat enough vegetables. And what you do eat, you don't burn off – assuming you're like the 40% of us who get no exercise. Most troubling of all, if you're like any parent of any child anywhere in the world, you may be passing your health habits to your children, which explains why **experts fear that this generation of American kids may be the first ever to have a shorter life span than their parents do.**

By too many measures, America is a lot less healthy than a developed nation has any business being.

We can go on and on and on…

Everyday I experience at least a few things that make me feel like I live in an undeveloped country, or worse!

Are you ready to "restart education" in America?

Lesson # 10 – Facts to be Verified by Independent Investigation

1. What was the plight of Blacks in 1865 to present?

2. What was the role of education in the advancement of Blacks?

3. What is the present status of American students in comparison to the rest of the Global Society?

4. Who will benefit from a better educational system?

5. Is there a relationship between education and the economy?

Part #1 - Final Facts to be Verified by Independent Investigation

1. Is "Race" a modern idea?

2. Did slavery predate race as an American creation "to enslave people who looked similar?"

3. Were race and freedom were born together, "explaining why some people could be denied the rights and freedom that others took for granted?"

4. Was race used to justify social inequalities as natural?

5. As the race concept evolved, was it used to justify 1) the extermination of Native Americans; 2)the exclusion of Asian immigrants and 3) and the taking of Mexican lands?

6. Were racial practices institutionalized within government, laws and society?

7. Do human subspecies exist?

8. Are there separate subspecies or races?

9. Are differences between groups only surface?

10. Is skin color only skin deep?

11. Is most variation within not between "races?"

12. How can race not be biological but racism still be real?

13. Is race a powerful social idea that gives people different access to opportunities and resources?

14. Have our government and society created advantages to being White?

15. Can privileges affect everyone, whether we are aware of it or not?

16. Will colorblindness end racism/bigotry?

17. Is pretending racism doesn't exist the same as creating equality?

18. Can racism be combated by identifying and remedying social policies that give advantages to some groups at the expense of others?

19. Is race enduring as a heartbreaking problem of American society and always has been since the first slaves arrived in North America?

20. Is it the American struggle to deal with the illusion of race and the power of that illusion?

Lessons Learned-Challenges Earned

Well, we have done our part.

What we choose to do with this information will determine the future of us all!

I, like all Americans, have an investment, what we do with this information; will determine our future, the future of our children and our grandchildren and everybody who call themselves Americans!

Let me summarize what I hope the "10 Lessons" have imparted and what the second part can do for you and me…

We are at the point where I hope you understand that "the jig is up!" There is no White people, no Black people, no Yellow people, no Red people; just people with different histories, different experiences, from different locations who live and love America.

We are all at a crossroads, just like when the ex-slaves left slavery and entered a hostile, foreign world and decided to hold on to two things: religion and education. Those two things served them well.

Now together as one, we must make a decision as we face a hostile and foreign economic society. I propose that "education" is still the way. (I'll only argue the case for education and leave the case for religion to others!)

Education is not new but the kind of education we offer must be different. Change is hard, it's hard to give up one way and grab hold on to a new way. We can choose to perish in disbelief or meet the new challenges and work together for the victory of all!

In my opinion there are two major changes that have to take place: the previous "superior" group must wipe that fake arrogance off their faces and "get to learning." The previous "inferior" group must wipe that fake victim-smile off their faces and "get to learning."

The new non-racial America belongs to the "learning."

And there ain't no learning in them schools now...

In this next section, I will share my understanding of how the mis-information highlighted in the Ten Lessons are played out in our schools today and what we must do to "restart" education with different principles and truths.

What an incredible time to be at this crossroads and have the wonderful opportunity to face the challenges that we never thought we would face in our lifetime!

PART 2

The Educational "R" - evolution

How to Restart Education in a Non-Racial America

"If an unfriendly power had attempted to impose on America the mediocre educational performance that exists today, we might well have viewed it as an act of war. As it stands, we have allowed this to happen to ourselves. We have even squandered the gains in achievement made in the wake of Sputnik challenge. Moreover, we have dismantled essential support systems which helped make those gains possible. We have, in effect, been committing an act of unthinking, unilateral educational disarmament."

-A Nation at-Risk, 1983

1983 –America's students rank in the World - #5

2009 – America's students rank in the World -#31

SECTION 1
THE GOAL FOR EDUCATION

To Survive and Thrive in a Smart and Successful America

The goal for America at this point in time is to restore America's **educational** and **economic** standing for a smart and successful America for us today and generations to come.

For that to happen, America has to make great changes in those two areas. We are going to concentrate on the changes that have to be made in the educational system which will consequently, powerfully, and positively affect the economic segment.

This section is going to be very brief, to the point, and hopefully simple to understand.

Let's get started!

STEP #1

Identifying the "Problem"

The U.S. School System that has Earned our #31 Position in the World:

This is based on my observations of over a half century in America that went from a Black America and a White America to an America where the black/white signs were removed but the system was not dismantled, was left in place, with "invisible" and "institutionalized" rules that have now left America in a really bad place for everybody.

It will take a group of smart, honest, and intelligent individuals ready to fight for our country to restart our educational system for a smart and successful America, again.

The Way Things are in the Present School System (for most schools, there are a few exceptions, i.e. Steve Perry's Capital Preparatory Magnet School in Hartford, Connecticut is probably the best example):

Johnny & Josie can't read, write, compute or think critically because that is not the goal of America's school system today.

The purpose of the American schools based on how they do business is to sort students and provide activities accordingly. The standard for sorting is the normal bell curve. A normal bell curve system standardizes mediocrity and bars excellence. Teaching and learning are not allowed.

Let's take the word "potato" to demonstrate how a "bell curve skool" operates. At the end of the school year the students take a norm based (bell curve) test where the item would appear like this: Question – Choose the correct spelling for an edible starchy tuber/ Answer – A, B, C, or D. All of the students' scores on the test will be placed on the normal bell curve and rated according to "race."

The students who place in the front of the curve will be the top group and they will be rewarded with accolades, awards, encouragement, support, superior labels, etc. The middle group gets the "average" treatment; and the bottom group gets labeled slow, stupid, at-risk and get to participate in demeaning activities where they are despised along with their parents and their "race."

While none of the students may really know how to spell "potato" the answers are provided so the probability is high that a percentage of students will select the correct answer. The odds are in favor of the "Asian/White" test takers.

The Worst Thing About Today's School

The Teaching Staff

The teachers are "products" of the school system that got us to the #31 place in the world. However, because we feel that we are still #1, the teachers are arrogant, egotistical individuals with inadequate skills, protected by "the system," and perpetuate the cycle that has brought us from #5 in 1983 to #31 in 2008/09.

> *Recommendation in A Nation at-Risk, 1983: The teaching profession should be strengthened through higher standards for preparation and professional growth*

The Certification

The system seems to be designed to keep out good teachers and certify "mediocre" ones. Teachers who are good at taking classes, accumulating credits looking for a secure job do well in the area of certification. People with compassion for students and want to keep their jobs based on the progress of their students and not blaming outside forces for the quality of the students, cannot get "certified."

The Curriculum

The curriculum seems to be a hodge-podge of subjects that is based on curriculum developed and "revised" from a century past. The data shows that students with all of the advantages/high expectations do not reach their potentials as well as the rest of the students leave school not really prepared.

> *Recommended in A Nation at-Risk, 1983: Graduation requirements should be strengthened so that all students establish a foundation in five new basics: English, mathematics, science, social studies, and computer science.*

The Students (Product)

There are mainly two types of students, those students who "hate" school and only go because they have to, or those students who hate it but they endure because they are really motivated to "get an education" no matter what and tolerate it as something they have to do to reach a particular goal like becoming a doctor or a lawyer, etc.

> *Recommended in A Nation at- Risk, 1983: We must demand the best effort and performance from all students, whether they are gifted or less able, affluent or disadvantages, whether destined for college, the farm or industry.*
>
> *"Our recommendations are based on the beliefs that everyone can learn."*
> *"That everyone is born with an "urge" to learn which can be nurtured."*
>
> *"That a solid high school education is within the reach of virtually all."*
>
> *"And that life-long learning will equip people with skills required for new careers and for citizenship."*

The Morale

The students hate it, the teachers hate it and the administrators become administrators so they don't have to teach anymore and they can earn more money and get as far away from children as they possibly can.

A School Day

A typical school is very short but seems like eternity. It's amazing that the President in his pre-roll out of his education plan is proposing to increase the school day and possibly year. The President says his own daughters and family are not very happy about the idea of increasing the time at school. Increasing a day that students already do not like is not a good thing. Doesn't the President understand that there is something wrong with this picture. Children are born wired to learn. If children don't like school something is wrong with school. He is paying approximately $30,000 per child and his daughters aren't having any more "fun" at school than the children at the Title I/No Child Left Behind Schools where a day at school is probably the worst place to be for any period of time. Here we go again, trying to "fix" something before you understand what's wrong with it! Lengthening the day should become an issue after all of the major things that are wrong with school are fixed. School in the "good ole days" was a place where children loved. If children don't like school, doesn't that tell you that something has got to be wrong with the people and what's going on there? Children love going to Steve Perry's school.

The President's eight year old daughter thinks that a 3-day holiday from school is right there with her father winning the Nobel Prize and celebrating their dog's birthday. There is no "teaching" and the "learning" that's going on is to "hate learning." Schools make "learning" something to hate!

> **Recommendation in A Nation at-Risk, 1983: The amount of time students spend engaged in learning should be significantly increased.**

Grading

If a students starts out not knowing anything about the subject matter; his first "testings" are probably not going to be good and certainly not like the student who may come into the class with more background knowledge on the subject. Let's say the first student studies very hard and increases his knowledge by 100% his grade will probably not get him an "A" in this course. However, the second student will increased his knowledge by 25% he is able to get an "A" in the class. This grading system does not motivate greater acquisition of knowledge or hard work for either student.

While scores go down, grades are going up in the US schools.

> **Recommendation in A Nation at-Risk, 1983: Schools and colleges should adopt higher and measurable standards for academic performance.**

Homework

Has anybody looked into the "purpose" or "value" of homework in the past fifty years? Homework is not good for anybody. The teacher in most cases is "forced" to give it and figuring out what to do with the work is "traumatic" as well as guilt-producing. Fear of students finding out that all that work was a waste of time is always in the air.

Proponents of homework claim that the purpose of homework are as follows: 1) reinforce what students learn in the classroom; 2) prepare them for further learning; 3) support the development of good working habits; 4) help build their sense of independence and personal responsibility and; 5) enhance communication between parents, students and schools.

I really hate to have to tell you, this is not what is happening. Homework is a source of grave pain in the homes where homework is considered important. Parents and students are "suffering." In many cases, "parents are doing the homework, the science fair projects and anything else that teachers assign for completion at home." The students of parents who are not capable of doing the child's work, then the homework is just totally ignored or adds to the hostility felt towards anything "school-related."

These are the following things that I feel apply to homework:

1. Children hardly ever, or never "recognize" the work at home, they don't know how to do it, they claim they have

never had it in school and it's up to the parents to figure out how to do it

2. The homework takes up too much time and makes the child more hateful of anything related to school

3. Engaged parents, in many cases end up doing it: I know a middle class family where the mother is a doctor and the father is a businessman and they have a nanny in the house. The family is motivated to do everything possible to have the children do well in school. When school is out for the summer the parents and nanny are totally "exhausted" and feel they can breathe and have a life for a few months! The assignments usually take the child (with the help of the nanny) from shortly after getting home until she has to go to bed, then the mother continues the process until she has to go to bed and then the father is left with "instructions" to please type the child's assignment!

4. Or parents where they pay high tuitions or "super achievement-motivated" parents delight in this "suffering" because it makes them feel that they are getting their money's worth and their child is getting a great education!

5. There might be a place for homework in a better system but not in the present one.

I would generalize the follow negative realities related to homework:

1. Make students feel overburdened

2. Reduces access to leisure and family time

3. Promote cheating and shortcut

4. Compound the effects of socio-economic inequalities among students

5. More and more parents do not have the time or the interest in making homework a positive part of children's development

6.

PTA

What is the purpose of PTA, anymore? In my opinion it's just another reason to rationalize why certain students "are not ready to learn" and the school is off the hook because these people don't even attend PTA!

PTA is dead, useless and anything dead needs to be buried.

"Obstacles" to Addressing and Solving the Problem

There are some major obstacles that's blocking most people from dealing with the "education problem." To say anything negative about the "school system" is interpreted as being against "education." Nobody wants to be against "education, public education and definitely not teachers."

Teachers and Teachers Unions Are the Foremost Problem

The teachers and teachers' union capitalize on the phenomena where it is anti-American to say anything about teachers. Teachers have a stronghold on any attempt or effort to say anything about the school system that might result in their "entitled security." Teachers stand between America and "the system."

The teachers, in my opinion, have to accept some of the major blame for protecting a "school system" where they are a victim as well as everyone else. Teachers would be one of the the greatest benefactors of a change in the "system."

Teachers are "not the system." They are victims of this outdated and dysfunctional system. Teachers however are only concerned about their "jobs" and their job-security. In this economy no one blames anyone for wanting to protect their jobs but is America going to become the poster child of "an ignorant nation" to allow teachers to keep their jobs without facing any changes in "the system."

I believe teachers are afraid of any serious evaluation of the school system because many teachers are very insecure about their "smartness" or "intelligence." Many teachers have gone into teaching because they didn't think they were smart enough to go into anything else. Some think of the teaching profession as a good "supplemental job" that complements a husband who is considered the "main professional" and teaching is only a secure job that supplements the family's income. Some go into teaching for the summers off and generous holidays during the years.

Teachers will need to become a part of the solution rather than the problem. Right now the "system" is bad for them as well as the students and everyone else. However, they become a part of the problem by "protecting" the system. It is the "system" that needs to be restarted. The system at present actually makes the teachers one of the major victims of the system.

Teachers can't be happy working in this "system." Most are not, many are miserable, get no respect, are angry and work in a hostile environment where they work with students that they do not respect or experience any real satisfaction or success.

Teachers need to become leaders in the movement to improve the system. Teachers will have to be informed and understand the new principles that will restart the school system. In the old system teachers tend to want to "reform" the school system. Some teachers want to change the behavior of parents, change the entire society, and change the type and characteristics of today's students. They put the responsibility of the school system on the parents, students and the society.

Things that Immediately Need to be Done During the Period Between the Ending of the Old and the "Restarting Process" for the New School System

1. Stop saying America has the best educational system in the world

2. Start concentrating on the #31 status and exactly what that means

3. Do not start "reforming" the system until you have read the following information and know exactly what and why you are making "changes"

4. Stop all national, state or local "awards" of any kind, i.e. Teacher of the Year, Principal of the Year, School of the Year, Top Ten Schools in the country, etc; this causes confusion, gives mixed messages and minimizes the seriousness of the situation; pits one group against the other regarding "superiority/inferiority"

5. We have got to be serious, focused, have a clear and concise vision with commitment to achieving "the goal."

6. We have got to stop the glass half full and the glass half empty game. With a #31 ranking, the glass is completely EMPTY!!!

7. A bell curve standard is not going to help put anything in the glass!

8. We need everybody, every American child making a substantial contribution to the filling of the glass!

9. We have to give up our racial status!

10. If English is the language of school then everybody has to know how to speak English to be able to do well in school and consequently capable of contributing to the "reconstruction" of our country!

STEP #3

CALL FOR THE "R" EVOLUTION

Children always learn and the one thing that too many in today's school system learn is to hate anything associated with school. If schools call this learning then children don't want anything to do with "learning." Only after being out of school for a long time, can you get today's American to let themselves do anything associated with "school-learning." They have to "detox" from the "trauma" of the school experience.

If you think the case I'm giving is probably right will you be ready for "restart." If you are still in denial, still don't understand the truth or can't accept the truth about our students, our society and our place in the world academically, I would ask you to just step back, do no harm and let those who are able to accept "truth" and want to do something about it, step forward, let's begin!

The objective is to restart education to produce:

"Lifelong Students Who Love Learning"

This motto obviously tells you that I believe that the school system that we presently have is one where students want to get out as quickly as they can with as little learning as possible and if they are lucky they hope they won't ever have to be students again.

When children get the opportunity to work hard, enjoy "learning" and experience success they gain confidence, self-esteem; based on "performance."

As we begin, we have to be clear regarding what we truly believe and then move forward or not:

Choice #1

Do you believe that the U.S. students scores rank #31 in the global community?

Or

Choice #2

Do you believe that the U.S. has the best educational system in the world?

Choice #3

Do you believe that we are ranked #31 and that our educational system is the best in the world?

Interpretation of the choice that you make:

If you choose to believe #1, you are able to face the facts and are ready to do something about it! You are at the right place at the right time!

If you choose to believe #2, I'm sorry you are choosing to believe an illusion! One last attempt to convince you to change your mind: If a system is #1, wouldn't that mean that it produces the #1 product? How can a system be the #1 system in the world, but the product it produces ranks #31 in the world? #31 must be at the bottom of the bottom. (I personally can't list 30 industrialized countries so that means that some of the smallest, possibly some third world countries are now scoring better than the U.S.) I would like for you to review the Ten Lessons, do some research and hopefully you will arrive at a new conclusion.

If you choose to believe #3, this might be considered "delusions of grandeur." You are able to accept the fact that our students rank #31 but you can't accept where that places the system that produces that ranking. Try to apply logic to this dilemma. Believing we are #1 with a #31 ranking is not rational. One or the other is true, both cannot be true simultaneously. A belief that America is #1 is not based on facts. The #31 ranking is based on facts. Come on now, let's face facts and strive to make America's students #1 again!

For those of you who are "ready to move forward," let's get started!

The most substantial and consequential change that has to take place in "restarting" our educational system are the changes that have to be made as the "operating principles." At the beginning of this process, America must have this conversation on "RACE." An educational system cannot be based on a "non-scientific, man-made FALLACY." Is there a Black race and a White race? Is the White race innately superior? Is the Black race innately inferior? What role does "race" play in the "normal bell curve" used in standardized testing?

Once we get passed this educational breakthrough we can proceed to adopt "operating principles" that can "restart education" based on facts. The foundation of the new educational system is **"Teaching and Learning"** for human beings.

We have to admit that if it's not fun, nobody wants to do it! Somehow, the present school system operates under a principle that "if it doesn't hurt, if they don't hate it, we are not doing our job, we are not doing our job well."

Teachers must be taught how to "teach" children to have a positive and enthusiastic attitude toward "learning." Children must see the "joy" of learning for learning sake, as well as learning for the positive things it brings to the students' lives.

All of the "set asides," "preferences," and "privileges" that are institutionalized will be removed. Everybody has to "learn" and learn "well" to be judged by an "absolute system."

In the "new" school system that will "restart" education in America, schools will provide teaching and learning for all students. The testing will measure the teaching and learning. The results will not be based on a curve which inherently results in mediocrity. The results will be based on an absolute standard of measurement, which makes excellence achievable, measurable and expected. This expectation will not be solely for the top quartile but for all students, the entire population of students!

A "half glass" will not become the "target." (first it's a half glass, then a quarter glass will do because you can always re-calibrate the standard)

We really don't even know what our children will need to know in this new world. What we want to do is "teach" students how to "learn." How to enjoy learning and the "process" of learning rather than the old system where it's what you know, the result rather than the process. Can we stop the "hating" that schools are generating?

This is truly a call for a revolution – not a Black Revolution, nor a White Revolution but the Education Revolution for All. Throughout the history of Black people and White people in America we have never looked at a problem with both a "Black and White perspective" that can lead to a win-win solution for both Black and White. If this book is successful and the dialogue is opened, it is my hope that following that dialogue we can decide together that it is in our best interest to re-start education in America for both Black and White and truly make this country a land of the free and the home of the brave...

This can be done by giving students the opportunity to learn a body of knowledge and interest in learning areas that have relevance to their lives and the lives of others.

The principles governing the "restart" is presented and dedicated to a smart and successful America, the beginning of a truly great country!

"One should guard against preaching to young people success in the customary form as the main aim in life. The most important motive for work in school and in life is pleasure in work, pleasure in its result, and the knowledge of the value of the result to the community."

-- Albert Einstein

The Operating Policies for the New School System

1. A child is ready to learn, capable and eager to learn if he/ she speaks a language, i.e. English, Spanish, Black English Only, Arabic, signed language, computer-generated communication, or any other "language"

2. Children will learn in the following environment:
   - High expectation for All children
   - Respect for All children

3. Encouragement and Support (a Grading System that rewards Hard Work, Effort, Improvement; and Mastery) Therefore a student beginning with a 30 (F) can improve 100% to a 60, his grade will reflect his hard work, efforts and improvement to reach a standard of "100"

4. Where Teachers, School administrators, Superintendent and Board are evaluated by: 1) success of their students and a warm loving relationship between teachers, students and parents.

5. Testing will be done using an absolute system, not a norm-based bell curve system

6. School operates on the basis of teaching and learning with the following principles:

   - The paradigm for teaching and learning are based on the following "R's": respect, responsibility, relevance and rigor
   - All children are equal; there is no little you and big me
   - Children determine their own destiny; it's hard but it's fair; knowing that you face the consequences of your action is the key
   - There is no free lunch; no free pass for "at-risk" or "privileged"
   - You have to work for everything you get: this goes for teachers and students
   - You do have a choice; you can pay now or pay later; you can help your fellow students now to be the best they can be or you have to take care of them later in jail; after they take what you have

- You have to be twice as good as the next person to get the job you want in life

- You can be anything you want to be if you work hard enough for it

- Standards are absolute and measurable; not norm-based bell-curved

- You either know it or you don't (A or F)

- Schools are not evaluated by who comes in but what goes out

- Everybody is equal; nobody is any better than you but you are no better than anybody else

- There is only on kind of people: people

Specific Changes that Must Be Made

Changes Pertaining to Children:

WE MUST START WITH CHILDREN AT A YOUNG AGE

Children are born ready to learn, and learn they do! When they have learned how "talk" they are ready and capable of learning anything

KNOWLEDGE AND USE OF THE COMPUTER SHOULD BE IMMEDIATE

Learning is more effective when it is a hands-on process

TO LEARN, CHILDREN MUST SEE THE RELEVANCE OF WHAT THEY ARE LEARNING

One of the greatest barriers to learning is boredom, insignificance, and irrelevancy

LEARNING TASKS MUST BE MODELED ON COMPLEX AND CHALLENGING REAL-WORLD PROBLEM SOLVING

Dealing with personal budgets that quickly demonstrate the financial advantages of education is a great example

REWARDED FOR HARK WORK, NOT GRADES

CHILDREN NEED RESPECT, ALL CHILDREN

The bright students and the slow learners and all the children in between

To learn, children must have a high sense of self-worth, confidence to take the risks needed to learn from mistakes

HETEROGENEOUS GROUPING, WHERE EVERY MEMBER OF THE GROUP HELPS THE OTHER BECOME EVEN BETTER

Children learn better in a cooperative group setting and this is how the new work world is like, workers must know how to learn together and from one another

CHILDREN ARE PEOPLE IN PROGRESS AND LEARNING IS THEIR BUSINESS

ALL CHILDREN HAVE NEEDS AND SHOULD HAVE RESPONSIBILITIES

CHILDREN MUST BE UNDERSTOOD AS INDIVIDUALS

CHILDREN MUST BE CHALLENGED TO THEIR LIMITS

CHILDREN MUST BE HELD ACCOUNTABLE FOR THEIR WORK AND HELPED AS THEY NEED HELP

Changes Pertaining to Parents:

PARENTAL INVOLVEMENT IN THE FOLLOWING WAYS:

- Finding out from the schools specifically what they will learn each day
- Asking the schools for the relationship between what they are learning and what they need to become successful, productive and happy adults
- Looking at their children's books
- Show enthusiasm for an oral report from child on school – Was it fun?
- Visit the schools
- Motivating and supporting the idea of learning as central to the lives of children
- Not <u>pressure</u> to succeed, but a positive view of learning
- Demand hard work, high expectations, high standards and an honest view of the children's options
- Have faith in the CHILDREN
- Know that high expectations in Japan get met, while lower expectations in this country are not met

ALL OF THE CHILDREN MUST BE EDUCATED WELL, NOT JUST THE TOP 15 OR 20 PERCENT

100% - GRADUATION RATE, NO CERTIFICATES

70% - GO TO COLLEGE AND SUCCEED

15% - GO TO AND SUCCEED IN OTHER INSTITUTIONS OF HIGHER EDUCATION

10% - GO DIRECTLY TO HIGH SKILLED EMPLOYMENT (TRAINING RECEIVED AT THE CAREER EDUCATION

CENTERS, OR OTHER COOPERATIVE TRAINING PROGRAMS)

0% - GET LOW SKILLED, MANUAL WORK WITH LOW WAGES

5% - ENTER MILITARY SERVICE

POSITIVE ATTITUDE TOWARD LEARNING, NOT JUST AN UNPLEASANT INSTITUTIONAL EXPERIENCE EARLY IN ONE'S LIFE

PROFICIENCY IN COMMUNICATION SKILLS, VERBAL, WRITTEN AND COMPUTER-GENERATE

PROFICIENCY IN AT LEAST 1 FOREIGN LANGUAGE WITH LESSONS BEGINNING IN KINDERGARTEN (ENGLISH FOR BLACK LANGUAGE ONLY SPEAKERS)

BASIC AND HIGH LEVEL MATH, APPLICABLE TO LIFE EXPERIENCES, COLLEGE, HOME OR WORK

CLEARLY MEASURABLE RESULTS

Changes Pertaining to School Systems:

DEVELOP A SCHOOL SYSTEM BASED ON RESULTS; TO MEASURE SUCCESS NOT BY WHAT GOES INTO A SCHOOL, BUT BY WHAT COMES OUT

ALL ADULTS INVOLVED WITH CHILDREN EITHER HELP OR THWART CHILDREN'S DEVELOPMENT WHETHER WE INTEND IT OR NOT AND THE FOLLOWING THINGS ARE SYMPTOMS OF A SYSTEM THAT THWART CHILDREN'S DEVELOPMENT:

- Low achievement, no achievement, low expectations, boredom and "mental dropouts"
- Criminal offenses
- Teenage pregnancy
- Drop outs, expulsions, and suspensions
- Vandalism
- Uninvolved parents and an uninformed community
- Poorly trained employees
- Racial tensions
- Behavior problems, acting out
- Unhappy, unmotivated, frustrated and non-productive teachers

On the Role of Testing:

TESTS ARE NOT THE OBJECT OF EDUCATION AND A GRADE POINT AVERAGE IS NOT THE MEASURE OF A CHILD'S EDUCATION

Education is done with children, not to them. If children are taught properly their behavior will value high achievement and the grades will take care of themselves

SCHOOLS WE NEED TODAY

CHILDREN LEARN AND INTERESTING THINGS ARE HAPPENING THERE

PARENTS ARE INVOLVED AND INTERESTED

TEACHERS ARE CHEERFUL AND WORK HARD

CHILDREN AND TEACHERS LIKE EACH OTHER

PARENTS, CHILDREN, AND TEACHERS HAVE BECOME INVOLVED WITH THE SCHOOL AND WITH EACH OTHER

"THE SPIRIT OF THE PLACE IS CONDUCIVE TO LEARNING"

THE PRINCIPAL SETS THE SPIRIT FOR THE SCHOOL

GOOD SCHOOLS BELIEVE ALL CHILDREN CAN LEARN AND NEVER GIVE UP ON A CHILD

Some schools make learning painful and unpleasant, stifle curiosity, demand rote memorization, punish wonder, and make even sex education boring. Take a dropout who can hardly read or write and cannot find his country on a globe; but he understands every balletic nuance of Michael Jordan's drive to the basket, endless lyrics of the latest rap songs, and dances and knows how to operate in a complex criminal enterprise.

HIGH EXPECTATIONS ARE SET FOR EVERYONE

Students tend to learn as little or as much as their teachers expect

Some educators predetermine, predispose, predict, and promote failure in school for students

Low expectations are a signal that a teacher does not respect her students and they can easily become a self-fulfilling prophesy

TEACHERS MUST BE ACCOUNTABLE FOR TEACHING

CHILDREN MUST BE ACCOUNTABLE FOR LEARNING

LEARNING IS AN ACTIVE PROCESS OF QUESTIONING, EXPLORING AND UNDERSTANDING

A CHILD IS NOT A RECEPTACLE TO BE FILLED WITH LECTURES AND MEMORIZED FACTS

The school day is not filled with talking teachers, tests, worksheets, assignments to be copied from the chalkboard and passive learning in general which leads to apathy and boredom

ACTIVE PARTICIPATION BY STUDENTS WITH CRITICAL THINKING A KEY COMPONENT

SCHOOLS ARE COMMUNITIES

The children are at the center and teachers function as coaches, discussion leaders, and advocates

STUDENTS ARE TREATED AS THE MOST IMPORTANT ASSET IN THE SCHOOL AND PROGRAMS EXIST THAT MAKE MAXIMUM USE OF THE STUDENTS

PROGRESS IS MEASURED NOT IN TEST SCORES, LESSON PLANS FILED, PAGES COVERED IN THE BOOK, ASSIGNMENTS PASSED OUT AND PAPERS GRADED

THE "CHILD" IS MORE IMPORTANT THAT THE "CLASS"

The child must not become a set of numbers on a file card. Every child should get some of the teacher's undivided attention; and children do badly in class mainly because they do not work hard, and they stop working hard because if they believe that no one in the system cares about them or what they do

CHILDREN MUST BE CARED FOR, RESPECTED AND RECOGNIZED THAT THEY EXIST AND MATTER

Some teachers may have learned to ignore and even despise children who fail or misbehave and their reactions may be colored by cultural differences or outright racism

196

Some teachers begin to look through the children, take their failures for granted, dismiss them as already lost and not worth caring about

Children many times get their first taste of "disrespect" in school

CHILDREN MUST BE TREATED AS MORE IMPORTANT THAN THE CONTENT OF THE COURSE

THE FIRST PRIORITY IS NOT LEARNING FACTS, BUT LEARNING HOW TO LEARN

CHILDREN DO BEST WHEN LEARNING IS INTERESTING AND FUN !!

CHILDREN MUST GET THE MESSAGE, A DOZEN OR MORE SIGNALS EVERY DAY THAT THEY ARE IMPORTANT AND WORTH SOME EFFORT

TRUE RESPECT FOR CHILDREN INCLUDES HOLDING THEM TO THE HIGHEST STANDARDS THEY CAN ACHIEVE

The enemy is mediocrity, and his allies are indifference, cynicism and despair

STUDENTS ARE REGARDED AS ACTIVE PARTNERS IN THEIR OWN EDUCATION

The Vision

All children (100%) ready for a happy, constructive, ethical and productive life

The Strategy

Graduation Requirements:

1. Calculus (algebra I required by 8th grade)
2. Fluency in a second language (beginning in kindergarten)
3. Well written (grammar, research, appropriate documentation, interesting, logical) 25 paged paper typed by the student using a word processing program and paper checked by a writing program (this paper begins in kindergarten, updated at the end of primary, elementary, middle and the middle of high school, the perfect paper by GRADUATION
4. Computer-functional, beginning in kindergarten
5. High and realistic goals that represent respect and compassion for self and all humanity

Operating Policies

*   A child is ready to learn, capable and eager to learn if he/she speaks a language, English, Spanish, Gullah, Arabic, signed language, computer-generated communication, or any other "language"
*   Children will learn in the following environment:
    1. High expectation
    2. Respect (multicultural curriculum)
    3. Encouragement and support (Grading system must reward hard work, effort; improvement; and mastery)
*   Where teachers, school administrators, and superintendent and Board are evaluated by
    1. Success of their students (using the above strategy list as criteria)
    2. Elimination of "downward variation"
    3. Parental involvement

4. Community support
5. Warm loving relationship between teachers, students, and parents

- Criterion-based testing; not norm-based

SECTION 2
Restarting Education with the new 4-"Rs"

FIRST "R" – RESPECT

RESPECT

The first "R" in the "R – evolution" is "Respect." Respect for the learner, not his race, or his family or his economic status. Every child is capable of learning if the "teacher" is ready and capable of teaching.

There will be no "pre-judging." Every student will be given the appropriate "respect" that he is capable of learning to the extent and ability of the "teacher."

DRESS CODES FOR TEACHERS! Could teachers show respect for the learners by dressing like they are going to do an important job – TEACH!

If a teacher isn't a good teacher, the least that they can do is not to make students hate school, hate anything that resembles a "teachable moment" and think less of themselves.

There is not one group of students that teachers do a better job than another, when you look at how every group is faring at present.

The gifted group is not achieving up to their expectations, the middle group is stagnant and steadily losing ground and the bottom group just drops out in huge numbers! No group of students/learners is given any respect in the present school system.

The present school system "likes" the students that come from families that presents to the school a well-behaved student with the right credentials: White, two-parent family, reading or close to reading, parents come to PTA, volunteer for everything, and sends nice gifts at holidays. The student is not personally "respected" and the school exploits that student who succeeds in spite of the system, not because of the system. Just a little "respect" to this student would manifest into a magnificent student that would reach, not only equal but exceed the accomplishments of his/her parents.

The lack of "respect" by this present school system decreases as the right characteristics decrease. By the time we get to the Black student, speaking Black Language Only, one parent family, "no parental involvement" and does not know how to read, shows no interest in reading and misbehaves in class, there is absolutely no respect for those students/learners.

Every student needs and deserves "respect" to achieve their greatest level of achievement.

SECOND "R" – RESPONSIBILITY

RESPONSIBILITY

Who is responsible for "teaching" and "learning?" THE TEACHER is responsible for the learning that takes place in and out of school!

The most important qualification for a teacher is that he is able and willing to teach. What most teachers require is a certain student before they are willing to teach!

Some teachers engage in "activities" and consider that as teaching. I took a course in computer programs and I got an A because I did all of the exercises well. After the class I was right where I was before the class.

That is not "teaching."

Having "certifications" do not mean that you are certified to "teach." It means that you were able to pass the exercises in class, as I did and then they repeat the "activities method" when they become the teacher.

More testing is needed of "teachers." Teachers who are not knowledgeable about their subject area use methods such as "bullying," intimidations, and "revenge" toward students who question the knowledge/lack thereof of the teacher.

The progress or lack thereof of students is the assessment/evaluation of the "teacher." If a student has not learned, a teacher has not "taught."

Bringing into the classroom the social issues of the community or the family is often used as an "excuse" or "get the teacher free of accountability" regarding the progress of the students.

Have you heard recently that most students today do not know the name of the first President of the United States? If they can't teach that anymore, what can they teach?

The school system is responsible for the #31 ranking that we have today!

All children are born achievers. Teachers tend to work miracles with the bright students but the others they don't seem to do very well and they take no responsibility for those students.

Become A Be Rather Than a Have

Examples of the *BE* teacher is: I will be a great teacher.
I will be a great example
I will BE a proactive person.
I will BE what I ask my students to be.
I will BE an excellent teacher every moment every second.
I will BE a circle of influence.
I will BE a producer.
I will BE a paradigm shifter when needed.
There can BE no friendship without confidence.
There can be no confidence without integrity.

Examples of the **have** teacher.
I will become a better teacher when **I have** brighter students
If only **I had** better students
If only **I had** more materials
If only **I had** more obedient student
If only **I had** more motivated students
If only **I had** more motivated, caring parents
If only **I had** a better principal and better co-works

Are you a *Be* or a *Have*?

Teachers Must Accept the Following:

1. You cannot teach what you do not know

2. "Proof is in the pudding" –what counts is what goes out of your class

3. Today's school system put our Nation at-Risk and is a substantial part of the cause and effect (responsible) for today's crash

4. What you want children to know; you have to teach (parents help would be wonderful, family's economic system would be great) but ultimately you have to "teach" what you want

the child to know (you are the only one paid to do this job)

5. It's learning, not learned (children need to love learning, the process)

6. Success in the 21st Century will be based on teaching & learning

7. The bell curve route will only lead to "standardized mediocrity"

8. All children can learn

9. All teachers can learn how to teach

10. All children are lovable and capable

11. There is only one race, the human race

12. The urge to learn is a part of being human

13. Effective teachers teach with an understanding that children alone hold the key to their minds

14. Do you believe we are born smart or do we get smart? The answer is hard work pays off

15. A fixation on ability is producing kids who give up easily and artful dodgers who would rather look smart than learn

This is a special message to teachers:

- Teach, every day
- Teach the curriculum
- Teach all
- Teach well (and still re-teach)
- Teach with caring, their success is your success

The 1983 report recommends:
They recommend that significantly more time be devoted to learning the New Basics. This will require more effective use of the existing school day, a longer school day, or a lengthened school year.

Implementing Recommendations are:

1. Instruction in effective study and work skills, which are essential if school and independent time is to be used efficiently, should be introduced in the early grades and continued throughout the student's schooling

2. The time available for learning should be expanded through better classroom management and organization of the school day

3. The burden of teachers for maintaining discipline should be reduced through the development of firm and fair codes of student conduct that are enforced consistently, and by considering alternative classrooms, programs, and schools to meet the needs of continually disruptive students.

4. Attendance policies with clear incentives and sanctions should be used to reduce the amount of time lost through student absenteeism and tardiness

5. Placement and grouping students, as well as promotion and graduation policies, should be guided by the academic progress of students and their instructional needs, rather than by rigid adherence to age, "race," social status or "aptitude" testing.

Persons preparing to teach should be required to meet high educational standards, to demonstrate an aptitude for teaching, and to demonstrate competence in an academic discipline. Colleges and universities should be judged by how well their graduates meet these criteria.

This is the way that I would simply put it. Making things simple, simply makes it work in my opinion. We only need people who really want to be a teacher, can pass a test of basic facts and understanding, love children (all children); believe that respect is reciprocal, from both sides, teacher to student and student to teacher. Just because you have a title doesn't mean that you can disrespect a student but expect the student to respect you, no matter what. The most important thing for a teacher is to have this understanding that teachers may fail to teach, but students never fail to learn and we don't give up on any student until they learn what you want them to learn. Student successes are the teachers' successes and students failures are your failures.

The last part of this is: teach and then test.

THIRD "R" – RELEVANCE

RELEVANCE

The Recommendations from 1983 needs to be put in place:

6. The teaching of English in high school should equip graduates to:

   A. Comprehend, interpret, evaluate, and use what they read

   B. Write well-organized, effective papers

   C. Listen effectively and discuss ideas intelligently

   D. Know our literary heritage and how it enhances imagination and ethical understanding, and how it relates to the customs, ideas, and values of today's life and culture

7. The teaching of Mathematics in high school should equip graduates to:

   A. Understand geometric and algebraic concepts

   B. Understand elementary probability and statistics

   C. Apply mathematics in everyday situations

   D. Estimate, approximate, measure, and test the accuracy of their calculations

   E. These standards should apply to those attending college as well as those who do not plan to continue their formal education immediately

8. The teaching of Science in high school should provide graduates with an introduction to:

   A. The concepts, laws and processes of the physical and biological sciences

   B. The methods of scientific inquiry and reasoning

   C. The application of scientific knowledge to everyday life

D. The social and environmental implications of scientific and technological development, for the college bound and those not intending to go to college

9. The teaching of Social Studies in high school should be designed to:

  C. Enable students to fix their places and possibilities within the larger social and cultural structure

  D. Understand the broad sweep of both ancient and contemporary ideas that have shaped our world

  E. Understand the fundamentals of how our economic system works and how our political system functions

  F. Grasp the difference between free and repressive societies

  G. An understanding of each of these areas is requisite to the informed and committed exercise of citizenship in our free society

10. The teaching of Computer Science in high school should equip graduates to:

  C. Understand the computer as an information, computation, and communication device

  D. Use the computer in the study of the other basics and for personal and work-related purposes

  E. Understand the world of computers, electronics, and related technologies

11. Achieving proficiency in a "other languages" ordinarily requires from 4 to 6 years of study and should, therefore be started in the elementary grades. We believe it is desirable that students achieve such proficiency because study of "other languages" introduces students to non-English speaking cultures, heightens awareness and comprehension of one's native tongue, and serves the nation's needs in commerce, diplomacy, defense and education

12. The high school curriculum should also provide students with programs requiring rigorous effort in subjects that advance students' personal, educational, and occupational

goals, such as the fine and performing arts and vocational education. These should be considered the basics, too

13. The curriculum in the crucial eight grades leading to the high school years should be specifically designed to provide a sound base for study in those ad later years in such areas as English language development and writing, computational and problem solving skills, science, social studies, "other languages" and the arts. These years should foster an enthusiasm for learning and the development of the individual's gifts and talents

A Practical List of Goals and Objectives for Every Child in Every School System

- Every child learns to read at a level where he can read the newspapers and comprehend its contents
- Every child learns to add, subtract, multiply, divide and understands what computation is necessary, and when

- Every child knows the major concepts of the sciences

- Every child has the knowledge of the major historical events from world, American and local history

- Every child knows the major geographical facts about the world, the United States, your home state and locally

- Every child can communicate verbally and in writing using standard English through letters and on the phone

- Every child feels he is lovable and capable and shows respect for himself, his family and all humanity

- Every child learns a language other than English (for Black Language Only speakers, English will be their other language)

- Every child has an appreciation for the arts

- Every child is healthy, physically, mentally and morally

- Every child knows good nutritional eating needs and its value

- Every child understanding the concept of a global society by keeping abreast of all current affairs, international, national, state and local
- Every child prepares for life after high school
- Every child attends school in a safe, clean and healthy environment
- Every child has safe, dependable, and clean transportation
- Every child has a plan: college, technical school, military or work/entrepreneurship
- Public education through adult education is available for life

FOURTH "R" – RIGOR

RIGOR

Is the glass half full or half empty? It doesn't really make a difference if a full glass is the objective!

If you are only interested in fake optimism, delusions of grandeur or bell curve standards, then the half full, half empty difference is relevant!

A Bell curve standard is incapable of "rigor."

Rigor is based on hard work, an absolute target and the possibility of everyone reaching it or not reaching it, equally!

The 1983 report recommended:

Recommended that schools, colleges and universities adopt more rigorous and measurable standards, and higher expectations, for academic performance and student conduct, and that 4-year colleges and universities raise their requirements for admission. This will help students do their best educationally with challenging materials in an environment that supports learning and authentic accomplishment.

1. Grades should be indicators of academic achievement so they can be relied on as evidence of a student's readiness for further study

2. four-year colleges and universities should raise their admissions requirements and advise all potential applicants of the standards for admission in terms of specific courses required, performance in these areas, and levels of achievement on standardized (no, not these bell curve standard tests!) tests in each of the five Basics and where applicable, foreign languages.

3. (not Standardized bell curve) tests of achievement should be administered at major transition points from one level of schooling to another and particularly from high school

to college or work. The purposes of these tests would be to: (a) certify the student's credentials; (b) identify the need for remedial intervention; and (c) identify the opportunity for advanced or accelerated work. The tests should be administered as part of a nationwide system of State and local (not standardized bell curve!) tests. This system should include other diagnostic procedures that assist teachers and students to evaluate student progress

4. Textbooks and other tools of learning and teaching should be upgraded and updated to assure more vigorous content.

5. In considering textbooks for adoption, States and school districts should: (a) evaluate texts and other materials on their ability to present rigorous and challenging material clearly; and (b) require publishers to furnish evaluation data on the material's effectiveness.

6. New instructional materials should reflect the most current applications of technology in appropriate curriculum areas, the best scholarship in each discipline, and research in learning and teaching.

There are five keys to memory which is required for "rigor"

1. **confidence**
2. **desire**
3. **concentration**
4. **association**
5. **repetition**

EPILOGUE

Closing Letter – INVITATION TO A "R"- EVOLUTION

Dear Fellow Americans and Citizens of the World,

- I am so happy that we finally met, even if only in this manner! I hope that we will soon meet in person as you decide to join this Movement or ask for more information as you lean toward joining.

- That is the purpose of this book. I am recruiting for the Education Revolution to Restart Education in America so our country can return to greatness with economic prosperity, leadership and innovativeness!

- I hope I obtained my intent to give you all of the background information that I have at my disposal to encourage and hopefully compel you to sign up now as a recruit in the war against mis-information.

- Our country needs us now, the world needs us now! Where America goes, goes the world; a common belief that is now notably confirmed by the financial meltdown that we are experiencing globally.

- As a descendent of slaves in America I am very spiritual and believe that all forces that operate on our lives are not known or fully understood by man. I believe that this book, the "manual for the revolution" is the purpose for my life. As revealed throughout this book I was exposed to the experiences and information that only I have cherished as pieces of a puzzle and now present and offer as the "key" to unlocking the educational mystery as a part of the "renewing of America."

- At many times in the past, I thought it was time to start the Movement, but I didn't get the go-ahead from the "spirits". Now I know why. It was not the right time. Even last year would not have been the right time. It was not until the economic crash and following the swearing in of the forty-fourth President of these United States that I could write, not to Black people, or White people, but to fellow Americans!

- In this book while there is a great deal of reference to the "racially divided" past, this is necessary because it defines so much of what we are experiencing today. We must be aware of and understand some things of the past before we can ever straighten out the present. Now that we are one America, we are Americans gravely at-risk and face a common challenge!

- I hope we will travel along the same path; seeing the things I have witnessed and let us come to conclusions that might make this movement, to restart education in America, a success!

- Together we can do this! Thanks for choosing to travel this road with me. It is my prayer that we find Victory for ALL... We have got to FIGHT, BOYCOTT, PROTEST and use whatever means necessary to "restart our education system" to save our future!

- Let's let the journey begin!

Please be in touch,
Ms. Johnnie